Critical Guides to French Texts

24 Pascal: Pensées

Critical Guides to French Texts

EDITED BY ROGER LITTLE, WOLFGANG VAN EMDEN, DAVID WILLIAMS

PASCAL

Pensées

Second edition

John Cruickshank

*Formerly Professor of French
University of Sussex*

**Grant & Cutler Ltd
1998**

ISBN 0 7293 0410 8

First edition 1983
Second edition 1998

DEPÓSITO LEGAL: V. 4.016 - 1998

Printed in Spain by Artes Gráficas Soler, S.A., Valencia for
GRANT & CUTLER LTD
55-57 GREAT MARLBOROUGH STREET, LONDON W1V 2AY

Contents

Prefatory Note

In this study references to individual fragments from Pascal's *Pensées* are followed by two numbers, the first preceded by the letter 'L' and the second by the letter 'B'. 'L' followed by a number refers to the arrangement of the *Pensées* in L. Lafuma (ed.), *Pascal: Œuvres complètes* (Paris, Seuil, Coll. L'Intégrale, 1963). 'B' followed by a number refers to the arrangement in L. Brunschvicg (ed.), *Pascal: Pensées et opuscules* (Paris, Hachette, 1897). It should be noted that the wording of the fragments is not always strictly the same in Lafuma and Brunschvicg. The wording used here is that of Lafuma.

As regards quotations from works by Pascal other than the *Pensées*, these are taken from the Lafuma edition only and are followed by the letter 'L' and the appropriate page reference.

John Cruickshank died in 1995. The revisions for this second edition and additional suggestions for further reading have kindly been provided by Mr J.P. Short.

1 The Religious Context

Pascal is still widely regarded as one of the most intelligent and persuasive advocates of Christian ideas. The notes which he made towards the end of his life, and which were published after his death under the title of *Pensées*, are among the great classic statements of religious belief. Against a background of ideas saturated by Christian thought Pascal stands out clearly. He does so not because he dominated his contemporaries by opposing the ideas of the age, but rather because he expressed in concentrated and memorable literary form their highest spiritual and intellectual aspirations. It is also worth noting that he wrote as a layman not a priest, and as a mathematician not a theologian. This approach played a part in giving to the *Pensées* a character and a quality which enable them to speak today, with urgency and directness, to many twentieth-century readers.

Religious life in the opening years of the seventeenth century in France was characterized by the impact of the general European movement known as the Counter Reformation or Catholic Reformation. There were repeated and widespread debates on such questions as human goodness and original sin, reason and faith, the moral status of the pagan thinkers of Greece and Rome, the authority of the Bible. These are all issues which play a significant role in the *Pensées* and Pascal's thought has many of its roots in the Counter Reformation, showing considerable awareness of the major religious controversies of the first half of the century.

The seventeenth century began with a contentious religious and philosophical inheritance. On the one hand the Wars of Religion which broke out in 1562 had been waged, often with much savagery, until around 1594. They confirmed the deep split in Christendom between the Catholic and Protestant faiths. On the other hand the sixteenth-century Renaissance, with its rediscovery of the intellectual achievements of ancient Greece and Rome, presented a major challenge to all Christians of whatever faith. We shall see later that what might be called the 'critical' side of Pascal's *Pensées* is largely directed against the moral and philosophical consequences of the Wars of Religion and Renaissance scepticism.

The Wars of Religion were influential in forming Pascal's strong detestation of civil war. He describes civil war as 'le plus grand des maux' (L.94, B.313) and his attitude was no doubt strengthened by the spectacle of various civil disturbances during his own lifetime, together with the sporadic outbursts of fighting between 1648 and 1653 known as the Fronde. In addition, the religious wars naturally provided Christianity with, as it were, a bad press. In this way they offered one form of alleged justification for the so-called *libertinisme scandaleux* associated with the young noblemen grouped round Théophile de Viau in the early years of the seventeenth century. It is a form of libertinism which included blasphemy, obscenity and generally licentious behaviour. It was largely checked during Richelieu's orthodox and authoritarian reign as First Minister (1624-42), though it persisted in smaller groups such as that surrounding Gaston, duc d'Orléans, and among the 'Messieurs du Marais' who played a part in the rebellion of the Fronde.

It is, however, to Renaissance scholarship, rather than to the Wars of Religion, that we mainly trace the growth of libertinism and free thought. In this case we are dealing with the other main form of libertinism — *libertinisme érudit* — which entered France from Italy during the sixteenth century. This was a form of philosophical scepticism derived from Greek and Roman authors and which ranged from deism to more or less acknowledged atheism, but which was often accompanied by restrained expression, quite unimpeachable behaviour, and a high moral seriousness. Pascal, in the *Pensées*, has a good deal to say about pyrrhonists or rational sceptics. The scepticism of Montaigne was a strong influence in his day, and some of the best-known philosophical libertines among his contemporaries included La Mothe le Vayer, Gabriel Naudé, Saint-Evremond and Cyrano de Bergerac.

It is also due to the activities of Renaissance scholars that neo-

Stoicism became such a strong element in seventeenth-century philosophical and religious thought. The Stoics most admired and studied in the sixteenth and seventeenth centuries were such thinkers of the Roman world as Seneca, Epictetus and Marcus Aurelius. Stoic ethics, while not Christian in inspiration, taught that true virtue is conduct in accordance with the divine will and that such conduct alone brings happiness. It was a doctrine of high moral aspiration. It put much emphasis on willpower, the cultivation of inner moral strength, and a life lived in detachment from the changing values and fashions of the external world. Such austere moral teaching, indeed, had formed the minds of some of the earliest Christian converts. It is not inappropriate, therefore, that in the sixteenth and seventeenth centuries efforts should have been made by the neo-Stoics to bring Stoicism and Christianity into harmony with one another. The so-called 'pagan virtue' of thinkers like Epictetus was widely admired, and serious and prolonged attempts were made to christianize Stoicism and to use Stoic wisdom to support rather than confound Christian beliefs. Thinkers whose activities along these lines influenced early seventeenth-century religious thought included Justus Lipsius and Guillaume du Vair.

As we shall see later, Pascal argued against both forms of Renaissance inheritance. His opposition to both scepticism and Stoicism pervades the *Pensées*. It is set out most clearly, in terms of rejection of Montaigne and Epictetus, in a conversation with Le Maître de Saci as reported by Nicholas Fontaine. Fontaine's account is printed separately from the *Pensées*, among Pascal's *opuscules*, and given the title *Entretien avec M. de Saci sur Epictète et Montaigne*.

If the negative side of Pascal's defence of Christianity involves a rejection of scepticism and Stoicism, the positive aspect is a prolongation of the intense spirituality and Christian renewal associated with the Counter Reformation. The Counter Reformation was no doubt prepared for by the fifteenth-century spirituality associated with the Brethren of the Common Life and summarized in *The Imitation of Christ* by Thomas à Kempis. It blossomed as a form of Christian humanism in the late fifteenth and sixteenth centuries until temporarily eclipsed by the

Wars of Religion. When it took on a new impetus at the end of the century, the Counter Reformation contained two main elements of moral and doctrinal reform. It is often called the Catholic Reformation precisely because of its self-purifying zeal and its concern to remove the many abuses and evils that had grown up within the Church. This corruption not only involved the ignorance and loose living of many parish clergy and monks, the buying and selling of benefices, the sale of indulgences and the general exploitation of popular superstition. It also had to do with the worldliness of many Church leaders, the neglect of dioceses by absentee bishops, the lack of systematic provision for the religious training of parochial clergy, etc. These are features of the Catholic Church in the sixteenth century which had formed part of the justification for the Protestant Reformation though the main impetus of the Reformers remained a doctrinal one. The second element in the Counter Reformation was therefore a sustained effort to resist Protestantism by redefining traditional, orthodox Catholic dogma and by issuing disciplinary decrees designed to overcome abuses which were regarded as the outcome of faulty administration rather than, as so many Protestant theologians held, the inevitable result of wrong theology.

The two aims of this second element in the Counter Reformation had much preoccupied the Council of Trent which met in various sessions between 1545 and 1563 and which issued agreed *canones et decreta*. These laws and decrees met a good deal of official opposition in France and were only agreed to by the Church assembly there in 1615. Nevertheless, their influence had been felt in the country well before that date. The moral aspect, rather than the theological one, had a particularly strong influence and a movement of deep inner renewal, as well as of outer reform, grew in strength. The Catholic Reformation was under way and was strengthened by the intellectual, spiritual and literary gifts of several outstanding men. A line of development can be traced from François de Sales, through Bérulle and Saint-Cyran, to Pascal. These men, together with later religious thinkers of the century such as Bossuet, Bourdaloue and Fénelon, represent that striking conjunction of literary gifts and

overriding religious concern and commitment which is a distinctive feature of the *grand siècle* in France.

It would not be appropriate to write at length about François
de Sales, Pierre de Bérulle and Saint-Cyran. All three knew one
another and were influenced by one another's ideas. All three
also made an outstanding contribution to the new spirituality.
But we are only concerned here with those aspects of their
thought and activities which had an influence on Pascal. In
terms of religious ideas, the so-called 'devout humanism' of
François de Sales is not at all close to Pascal's own thought.
François de Sales, unlike Pascal, was educated by the Jesuits and
retained an interest in the philosophies of Plato and Aristotle, as well as having a close knowledge of the Latin poets.
Later he was strongly attacked by the Jesuits and this is an experience which he shared with Bérulle, Saint-Cyran and Pascal
himself. He was an indefatigable preacher and reforming bishop
of Geneva from 1602 until his death in 1622.

François de Sales believed that intense spirituality may be
achieved in everyday life. The third chapter of the *Introduction
à la vie dévote* is significantly entitled: 'Que la dévotion est con-
venable à toutes sortes de vocations et professions'. Pascal, born
a year after the death of François, was familiar with salesian
doctrine but would have had reservations about such a claim.
And he would not have accepted the humanist contention of
François de Sales that man has a natural inclination to love God
or that austerity and self-discipline can easily mislead the pious
('Gardez vos forces corporelles pour servir Dieu'). But there
could be no doubt about the total love of God which François
set out in his *Traité de l'amour de Dieu* of 1616. There is, too, a
mystical quality in this work which reflects another aspect of the
new spirituality. Indeed, the Catholic Reformation had been
given a significant impetus by the sixteenth-century tradition of
mystical piety which reached France from Spain through such
figures as Saint Theresa of Avila and Saint John of the Cross.

In terms of historical links, François de Sales is indirectly connected with Pascal in the sense that, during the last three years of
his life, he acted as spiritual guide and adviser to Mère Angélique Arnauld, abbess of the convent of Port-Royal (in fact

while she was carrying out the reform at the convent of
Maubuisson between 1618 and 1622). It was also through
François de Sales that Mère Angélique entered into a friendship
and correspondence with Jeanne de Chantal until the latter's
death in 1641. Madame de Chantal and François de Sales had
founded the order of Visitandines in 1610. The Visitation Order
was open to young women and widows unable to accept the
most severe discipline of the ordinary religious house but who
wished to devote their lives to gentle piety and the care of the
sick and the poor. Mère Angélique wanted to join the Visitation
nuns herself, but François de Sales dissuaded her and to this extent he was responsible for her continuing guidance at Port-
Royal until her death in 1661.

In view of the influence which Mère Angélique had on Port-
Royal, the central role of Port-Royal in the Jansenist movement
and the fact that Pascal was to have close relations with Port-
Royal, the connection between François de Sales and Pascal is a
real if oblique one. And it is also the case that the various
solitaires or *messieurs* — men of the world who came to live
retired lives close to Port-Royal without, for the most part,
changing their status as laymen and who sought spiritual perfection without entering a religious order — while they largely renounced their former lives 'in the world', nevertheless followed
the salesian teaching that the layman's life can be a school of
sanctity. There is general agreement that the first generation of
Port-Royal was faithful to the spirituality of François de Sales
though this situation became somewhat changed later under the
guidance of Saint-Cyran. But if it is something of an exaggera-
tion to describe François de Sales as 'un janséniste avant la
lettre', it is true that salesianism retained its influence on certain
individuals at Port-Royal, not least on Mère Agnès who was a
younger sister of Mère Angélique and who took her place as
abbess while Mère Angélique was at Maubuisson.

Both François de Sales and Pierre de Bérulle were regarded as
saints by Saint-Cyran during their lifetime. But whereas
François was officially canonized within forty years of his death,
Bérulle has never been declared a saint. However, he was
renowned for his outstanding personal piety and is often

described as the father of the French school of spirituality. He shared Saint-Cyran's taste for austerity and although he played some part in the political life of his day and was made a cardinal in 1627, he was far from being a worldly prelate. Again like Saint-Cyran, he was influenced by the teachings of Augustine though his Augustinianism remained more moderate that that of most Jansenists. In general, he looked upon the philosophy of Plato as an ally of Christianity and regarded Stoicism as an enemy.

Apart from his teaching and his personal example, Bérulle made a significant contribution to that practical side of the Catholic Reformation which consisted of the reform of religious houses and the creation of new orders of regular clergy which helped to lay the foundations of the new spirituality. He established the reformed Carmelite Order of Theresa of Avila in France and in 1611 he founded the Congregation of the Oratory, based on the foundation of Philip Neri in Rome, but adapted to French needs. The Oratory, as the name implies, emphasized the importance of prayer and was concerned to give dignity and piety to the priesthood. It also established colleges which soon opened their doors to those who had no priestly vocation. These colleges laid considerable stress on such scientific subjects as astronomy and mathematics.

Bérulle's religious thought emphasized the infinite nature of God and the finitude of man. This led him, in a way which anticipates Pascal, to attribute great importance to Jesus Christ as man's unique means of access to God. This 'Christocentrism', strongly shared by the Pascal of the *Pensées*, is expressed most memorably in Bérulle's *Discours de l'état et des grandeurs de Jésus* of 1623. This is a work to which, significantly, Saint-Cyran contributed and which he had translated into Latin by his cousin the Jansenist Martin Barcos. It is said that Pascal read Bérulle closely and indeed many of the latter's ideas are taken up again in the *Pensées*. For example, his view that human abasement is the only means of spiritual ascension, or his insistence on the dramatic dualism of human nature which renders it totally dependent on Christ for fulfilment: 'Voilà notre état et condition, état heureux et misérable; misérable en nous-mêmes,

heureux en autrui (Jésus-Christ)'. One recalls Pascal's question:
'Si l'homme n'est fait pour Dieu, pourquoi n'est-il heureux
qu'en Dieu?' (L.399, B.438).

If Bérulle's Christology is one of his main links with Pascal, a
less obvious but no less important link is his tragic view of the
human condition. As we shall see, this is an important element
in the *Pensées* and it is also, incidentally, a major reason for
twentieth-century 'existentialist' interpretations of Pascal.
Bérulle regarded human life as a journey to be travelled 'en
misère, en ignorance, en péché' and ended by the certainty of
death: 'Le monde est échaffaud de notre supplice, nous sommes
non seulement obligés à la mort mais condamnés à la mort'.
Pascal similarly finds the essence of men's condition in the fact
that they are 'dans les chaînes, et tous condamnés à la mort'
(L.434, B.199).

The roots of the Jansenist movement in France are to be
found in the spirituality of the Counter Reformation. Although
the term 'Jansenist' was not used until the 1640s, the reforming
zeal and austere piety associated with the movement really began
with the conversion of Mère Angélique and the transformation
of the convent of Port-Royal which she set in train after 1608.
We have seen that she was supported and advised by François de
Sales during the last three years of his life, and later, from about
1633 until his death in 1643, Saint-Cyran similarly had an increasingly close relationship with Port-Royal, eventually acting
as spiritual counsellor to the convent. Before his death, the
austere Augustinian doctrine which he shared with Mère
Angélique had become known as Jansenism and had come into
conflict with Richelieu and with prevailing religious and political
orthodoxies.

Jean Duvergier de Hauranne, who became abbot of Saint-
Cyran in 1620, is generally regarded as the founding father of
French Jansenism. He was the spiritual heir of François de Sales
and, more closely, of Bérulle. He was a student at the Sorbonne
and at Louvain where he had contact with the neo-Stoic Justus
Lipsius, and continued his studies with his friend Jansenius.
They spent a brief time in Paris and a longer period at Bayonne.
Both men read and meditated on Augustine with close attention

and considerable enthusiasm. Part of their purpose in studying this father of the Church, who lived in the late fourth and early fifth centuries, was to get behind the worldly accretions of the intervening period to the purity of early Christianity. They also intended to combat Protestantism with some of its own weapons since Luther had taken much from Augustine. They were particularly struck by Augustine's conviction of the utter powerlessness of man without God's grace, his belief that man is 'justified' by faith rather than works, and his assurance of the total sufficiency of Christ's sacrifice for man's salvation and of God's omnipotence as he chooses some for salvation and others for reprobation.

An important outcome of these ideas was a large work, the *Augustinus*, written by Jansenius and published in 1640 two years after his death. It was chiefly because of statements allegedly found in the *Augustinus* that Jansenists were accused of heresy or thinly disguised Protestantism. Already for a number of years both Jansenius and Saint-Cyran had in any case been regarded with considerable suspicion, and some dislike, by Richelieu. Like Bérulle, they held that political action should be guided by religious principles and they were critical of Richelieu's expedient alliances with Protestant countries and what they interpreted as his inclination to put the well-being of the state before that of the Church. Jansenius expressed his disapproval of Richelieu's policy in his *Mars gallicus* of 1635 and was supported by Saint-Cyran. In the year of Jansenius's death from the plague, 1638, Saint-Cyran was finally arrested by Richelieu and imprisoned in Vincennes for close on five years. He continued to give spiritual guidance to the nuns of Port-Royal in letters smuggled out of prison and wrote the *Lettres chrestiennes et spirituelles* posthumously published in 1645 and 1647. These letters contain the essence of French Jansenism (as distinct from the Jansenism of the Low Countries), at least in the first phase of its existence, and they helped to link the convent of Port-Royal (both the house in Paris and that outside Paris in the valley of Chevreuse) particularly closely to the movement. This link was further strengthened by the fact that while Saint-Cyran was in Vincennes the polemical defence of

Jansenist views was carried on in particular by Antoine Arnauld
— for example in his *De la fréquente communion*, published
with an introduction by Saint-Cyran's cousin Barcos in 1643 —
and the name of the Arnauld family was virtually synonymous
with that of Port-Royal.

As things turned out, Saint-Cyran died within a year of his
release from Vincennes. His death marks the end of the first
phase of Jansenism. This is the Jansenism which coloured
Pascal's own thought so strongly, though he himself was active
during the second phase lasting from Saint-Cyran's death until
the temporary truce of 1668, the so-called 'Peace of the
Church'. It was during this second phase that Pascal underwent
his 'first conversion' of 1646 in Rouen as a result of the efforts
of the Jansenist-inclined Deschamps brothers. It is significant
too that several of the Rouen clergy with whom he was in contact were friends or disciples of the late abbé de Saint-Cyran. It
was also during this period that Pascal attacked the Jesuits to
such purpose, and defended his friends at Port-Royal, in the
eighteen *Lettres provinciales* published between January 1656
and March 1657 and which constitute his other major work in
addition to the *Pensées*. As regards Jansenism itself, the movement underwent such sustained pressure and eventual persecution that it was a pale shadow of its former self after 1668. In
that year Port-Royal-de-Paris ceased to be associated with
Jansenism and the remaining (and original) major centre, Port-
Royal-des-Champs, was razed to the ground on the orders of
Louis XIV in 1711.

This is not the place to look in any detail at Saint-Cyran's
thought, but it is clear that his writings from prison find many
echoes in the *Pensées*. First among these is his Augustinian
emphasis on man's total wickedness because of Adam's sin and
his utter dependence on God's grace. Far from being naturally
free, man is a slave to concupiscence (the desire, originating in
the senses, for purely temporal and material ends) and only
God, if He so wills, can give man the grace to conquer concupiscence. This idea is repeatedly expressed by Pascal, as when
he writes that 'il n'y a pas d'autre ennemi de l'homme que la
concupiscence, qui le détourne de Dieu' (L.269, B.692), or when

he says of man that 'sans la grâce il est censé semblable aux bêtes brutes' (L.131, B.434). Augustine's emphasis on man's dependence on grace was a result of his controversy with the followers of Pelagius. Pelagianism taught that man can take the fundamental steps towards salvation unaided, or by his own strength, and rejected the idea of the transmission of original sin following Adam's fall. With the revival of Augustinianism in the sixteenth and seventeenth centuries the debate about freedom and about human nature was once again revived (as it had been in the Middle Ages). The Jesuit view of freewill, originating in a Latin work by the Spanish Jesuit Molina entitled *The Concord of Freewill with the Gifts of Grace* and published in 1588, was more or less a Pelagian one, and for many Jansenists Molinism was the main enemy. The conflict between Saint-Cyran and the Jesuits — a conflict of which Pascal's *Lettres provinciales* were another manifestation — was fundamentally one between pessimistic and optimistic views of man's purely human capacity to do good. We shall see later how Pascal used parts of these conflicting views, and indeed the very fact of an irreducible conflict between them, to argue the case for the truth of Christianity.

Many other ideas contained in Saint-Cyran's writings have a place in the *Pensées*. These include his emphasis on prayer and contemplation, his conviction that private spiritual needs must take precedence over the demands of society, and his attitude to war and the suffering — particularly for the poor — which it entails. Perhaps most generally characteristic of Jansenism is his preoccupation with self-inspection which is a means of becoming aware both of our own imperfections and of the stirrings of divine grace. Pascal, as so often, puts these two things into a relationship of interdependence and tension when he writes: '...il est également dangereux à l'homme de connaître Dieu sans connaître sa misère, et de connaître sa misère sans connaître le Rédempteur qui l'en peut guérir' (L.449, B.556).

2 The Man and the Book

The main facts of Pascal's life can be found in a variety of books. Nevertheless, it is worth providing a brief outline here not simply for convenience and completeness but because it will help to clarify the links between his life and the intellectual context of the age, as well as those between his biography and the *Pensées*. This is a case where knowledge of the man and the age throws considerable light on the book.

Blaise Pascal was born at Clermont-en-Auvergne (now Clermont-Ferrand) on 19 June 1623. His father, Etienne Pascal, was a successful lawyer who by 1625 presided over a court in the Auvergne with powers to oversee the tax system and to give legal judgments in disputed cases. On his father's side, then, Pascal was a product of the middle-class *noblesse de robe*. His mother, who died when he was three years old, belonged to the *bourgeoisie marchande*. In short, he came from that educated and moneyed section of the bourgeoisie which was rapidly rising to power at a time when the old nobility, the *noblesse d'épée*, was declining in influence.

Three Pascal children survived infancy: Blaise himself, his elder sister Gilberte, and his younger sister Jacqueline. Gilberte, who later married a cousin Florin Périer, was to write a brief life of her brother — most interesting if not always totally accurate — shortly after his death. Jacqueline entered the convent of Port-Royal in 1652 despite her father's initial opposition and as the result of a long-standing desire to become a nun. She provided an often close link between Pascal and this particular religious house.

In 1631 the family moved from Clermont to Paris. Etienne gave up his legal duties, set out to pursue his interests as a keen mathematician and amateur scientist, and took on total responsibility for the education of his three children. Blaise proved to be a particularly precocious child in intellectual terms and, if not quite the prodigy which Gilberte describes, made remarkably rapid progress, especially in mathematics. So gifted was his son, and so responsive to intellectual stimulation, that Etienne eventually took him from time to time to meetings of the scientific academy first grouped round Père Mersenne in 1635. The academy included, in person or by correspondence, such famous mathematicians and scientists as Roberval, Desargues, Fermat, and Descartes. All four, in different ways, had a significant influence on Pascal.

In 1640, when still just seventeen, Pascal published an *Essai pour les coniques* which demonstrated certain conic properties, showed his potential gifts as an outstanding geometer, and was designed as the prelude to a *Traité des coniques* which remained unfinished. As the years passed his intellectual curiosity and mental powers increased. Nevertheless, unlike many young intellectuals of the period, he does not appear to have been attracted by that *libertinage érudit* which he eventually sought to confound in the *Pensées*. Gilberte comments on this fact and tells us that Blaise attributed it to the influence of his father. At this time Etienne appears to have been a 'religious' man only in the sense that he fulfilled all formal religious obligations. But he made a distinction — apparently accepted by his son from a relatively early age — between objects of intellectual inquiry and objects of faith. Gilberte quotes Blaise as saying that his father held firmly to the maxim that 'tout ce qui est l'object de la foi ne le saurait être de la raison, et beaucoup moins y être soumis'. This distinction between knowledge and belief, and the readiness to grant legitimacy to both in their different spheres, is familiar enough. But it is fundamental in the sense that it was to remain at the core of Pascal's epistemology and served as the ultimate principle behind a series of distinctions made in the *Pensées* between *scio* and *credo* (L.7, B.248), between the *esprit de géométrie* and the *esprit de finesse* (L.511-13 and 751, B.1-4), and between the physical, rational and spiritual levels of the 'three orders' (L.308, B.793).

In 1639 Pascal's father was appointed commissioner for the raising of taxes in Normandy on behalf of the Intendant or senior royal agent for the area. The post was obviously not one calculated to endear Etienne to the local population, but by early 1640 the family was settled in Rouen and the next six or seven years were to prove to be among the most important in Blaise Pascal's life. It is the period during which he did much of his mathematical and scientific work and underwent what is often called his 'first' conversion through Jansenist influences. This event occurred in 1646 and marks the first practical effect on the Pascal family of the Catholic reform of the period. A Rouen curé, Jean Guillebert, had converted two members of the local gentry, the Deschamps brothers, to a Jansenist form of spirituality. They, in their turn, wished to give practical and charitable expression to their faith by offering their medical skills to others. They had become amateur bone-setters and were invited to treat Etienne Pascal who had dislocated a leg. In the end, they stayed for three months in the Pascal household and gradually converted the whole family, including Gilberte and her husband, from apparently orthodox, routine religious observance to a fervent inner faith in keeping with the teachings of Saint-Cyran and the new spirituality.

In the field of mathematics Pascal's pioneering work did much to lay the foundations of present-day calculus and probability theory. He carried on this work into the late 1650s. On the scientific side he invented a mechanical calculating machine (*la pascaline*) to aid his father's complicated fiscal computations. The first of a small number of such machines was constructed with the help of a Rouen mechanic in 1644 and eventually dedicated to the chancellor Séguier, one of the leading royal ministers. It was also around this time that Pascal began his important work on the vacuum and atmospheric pressure. Much later, less than eighteen months before his death, he was associated with the Duc de Roannez in setting up a system of cheap public transport in Paris. A number of public carriages, the so-called *carrosses à cinq sols*, first ran between the Luxembourg and the Porte Sainte-Antoine.

This short summary of some of Pascal's achievements points to several important conclusions. In the first place, it is now clear that Pascal's life cannot be neatly divided into an early scientific phase and a later religious one. His is not the story (generally current in the eighteenth and nineteenth centuries) of an outstandingly gifted mathematician who 'got religion' and unfortunately renounced all serious intellectual endeavour thereafter. We now know that his religious interests existed from a relatively early period and that his mathematical and scientific activities, often interrupted by severe ill-health, continued after both his first conversion of 1646 and the second, mystical experience of 1654.

Again, there is much evidence in Pascal's scientific work of his very practical qualities of mind. The *pascaline* or the *carrosses à cinq sols* are obvious examples of *applied* theory and a practical bent. Related to this is his repeated insistence on the need for scientists to prove by practical experiment rather than to accept the traditional authority of ancient writers such as Aristotle. This point is firmly made, for example, in his correspondence of 1647 with the Jesuit Père Noël. He asserts that experimentation must be the guiding principle of the physical scientist. The *Pensées* reflect a similar attitude which takes practicality even further. Pascal implies that mathematical and scientific theorizing — apart, no doubt, from those instances where it can be usefully applied to human well-being — is an activity distinctly inferior to the study of human nature. He writes, for instance: 'J'avais passé longtemps dans l'étude des sciences abstraites et le peu de communication qu'on en peut avoir m'en avait dégoûté. Quand j'ai commencé l'étude de l'homme, j'ai vu que ces sciences abstraites ne sont pas propres à l'homme, et que je m'égarais plus de ma condition en y pénétrant que les autres en l'ignorant' (L.687, B.144). He makes a similar point elsewhere when he writes that 'la science des mœurs me consolera toujours de l'ignorance des sciences extérieures' (L.23, B.67). It is clear, nevertheless, that Pascal's study of man and God in the *Pensées* is coloured by his mathematical and scientific activity. An obvious example, among several, is the famous fragment on the necessity for wagering on God's existence (L.418, B.233).

One other conclusion, prompted by Pascal's work as a mathematician and scientist, is related to his posthumous reputation. In the eighteenth and nineteenth centuries his work in these fields was much less influential than that of Descartes.

The latter's rationalistic mechanism had an enormous influence on European attitudes of mind throughout this period. However, scientific attitudes have greatly changed in the course of the twentieth century and Pascal is now seen to possess renewed relevance and importance as an early pioneer of the twentieth century's achievements in computer science and the mathematics of probability.

In September 1647 Pascal was visited twice in Paris by Descartes. But it seems that on a personal level neither man found the other particularly congenial. A major reason for this stay in Paris had been the seeking of medical advice. Pascal was strongly encouraged by the doctors to avoid overwork and to indulge in some relaxation and pleasure in the interests of his health. This is often taken by biographers as marking the beginning of Pascal's somewhat poorly documented 'worldly' period and associated with a temporary abatement of his religious fervour. In fact, we know that he made frequent visits (with Jacqueline) to Port-Royal during the winter of 1647-48 and it seems more likely that his 'période mondaine' lies between his father's death in 1651 and his second conversion of 1654. The lengthy letter written by Pascal to Gilberte on Etienne's death suggests no diminution of his faith, and indeed the 'worldly' element can easily be exaggerated. But we do know that he moved more frequently in some of the more fashionable social and intellectual circles in Paris during the three years 1652-54. In April 1652, in the home of the Duchesse d'Aiguillon, he lectured on his calculating machine and on the vacuum. He continued his scientific work and in June sent a machine to Queen Christina of Sweden. In 1653 he renewed his friendship with the Duc de Roannez who was then governor of the province of Poitou. This brought him into contact with two celebrated *libertins érudits* of the period, the Chevalier de Méré and Damien Mitton. Both were men of considerable intellectual gifts with whom Pascal had much in common. Both made an indirect contribution to the *Pensées*, not only because they represented the type of sceptical intellectual addressed by Pascal in his defence of Christianity, but because of Méré's ideal of the *honnête homme*, the humane and urbane all-round man (e.g. L.647, 605, 195, 732, B.35-8), and the interest of both men in the mathematics of gambling (e.g. L.158, 418, 577, B.236, 233, 234). There are also three direct references to Mitton in connection with the Augustinian/Stoic debate on human nature (L.597, 642, 853, B.455, 448, 192).

Jacqueline Pascal had entered Port-Royal early in 1652. In September 1654 Blaise admitted to her that despite his enjoyment of the social and intellectual life of Paris he felt the need to change his way of life profoundly. This change came, largely unbidden, in the dramatic spiritual experience which Pascal underwent on the night of 23 November 1654, the famous 'nuit de feu'. This event is attested by the 'Mémorial', a document written in Pascal's own hand on both parchment and paper and found sewn into his doublet on his death. Although not an integral part of the *Pensées* and not known to the public until the late eighteenth century, it is fundamental to an understanding of Pascal's interpretation of Christianity and is usually published as an addendum to the *Pensées*.

While the conversion of 1646 had been essentially a matter of intellectual conviction accompanied by spiritual concern, that of 23 November 1654 was a deep, mystical experience involving two fundamental features: a sense of direct union with God and absorption in the Godhead; a consequent knowledge and experience of God inaccessible to the intellect alone. It is inevitable that such an experience can only be expressed, at best, in enigmatic and elliptical terms. The first four lines of the 'Mémorial' read as follows:

Feu.
Dieu d'Abraham, Dieu d'Isaac, Dieu de Jacob,
non des philosophes et des savants.
Certitude, certitude, sentiment, joie, paix.

The vocabulary here is typical of the mystic, including the reference to fire or light which has both a sensory and a spiritual existence. The certainty and joy are those which come, as Pascal puts it in the *Pensées*, 'non par preuves de dehors, mais par sentiment intérieur et immédiat' (L.328, B. 732). The second line, which repeats God's definition of himself speaking to Moses from the burning bush (Exodus 3:6), is glossed by Pascal in the third line to emphasize his contention that true knowledge of God is not knowledge of an intellectual concept — the God of the philosophers — but of a God who is directly apprehended through the mystical vision, through faith, and through worship and prayer. The same point is made in a lengthy fragment in the *Pensées* which includes the following sentences: 'Le Dieu des chrétiens ne consiste pas en un Dieu simplement auteur des vérités géométriques et de l'ordre des éléments [the Cartesian God]... Mais le Dieu d'Abraham, le Dieu d'Isaac, le Dieu de Jacob, le Dieu des chrétiens, est un Dieu d'amour et de consolation; c'est un Dieu qui remplit l'âme et le cœur qu'il possède; c'est un Dieu qui leur fait sentir intérieurement leur misère, et sa miséricorde infinie; qui s'unit au fond de leur âme; qui la remplit d'humilité, de joie, de confiance, d'amour; qui les rend incapables d'autre fin que de lui-même' (L.449, B.556). It is hardly necessary to point out that this type of distinction presented Pascal with a fundamental problem in the *Pensées*. He had to employ largely rational discourse (the type of discourse which the *libertin* would understand) in making the case for a suprarational conception of God.

In January 1655 Pascal spent three weeks in a religious retreat at Port-Royal-des-Champs. It was at this time that he had the important discussion with Le Maître de Saci mentioned in the previous chapter. It was probably in the same year that he wrote his short treatises, *De l'esprit géométrique* and *De l'art de persuader*, and began his *Ecrits sur la grâce*. During this time the pressures against Jansenism had become intensified and Antoine Arnauld, the leading protagonist of Jansenism, was threatened with censure and conviction of heresy by the Sorbonne (then the theological faculty of Paris). Eventually Pascal was asked to write in defence of Arnauld and the Jansenist cause at large. He responded with his eighteen *Lettres provinciales* (and fragments of a nineteenth). They were published under a pseudonym during 1656-57 and display Pascal's considerable intellectual and literary gifts as a satirical controversialist. The Jesuits, with their anti-Jansenist bias and indulgent view of human nature, were the main object of his attack.

Although the *Lettres provinciales* are an important work of moral indignation and a monument of polemical art, they do not directly concern us in more detail here. But it is worth pointing out that the addendum to the *Pensées* which contains the 'Mémorial' also includes a number of notes developed in the *Provinciales* (e.g. L.954, 955, 956, 960, 979, B.925, 929, 928, 921, 945).

Pascal found time, in the midst of his campaign against the Jesuits, to write letters of spiritual direction during six months to the sister of the Duc de Roannez. Charlotte de Roannez wished to enter a religious order and received considerable encouragement from Pascal.

In March 1656 Pascal's niece, Marguerite Périer, was cured at Port-Royal of a long-standing eye ulcer by contact with a relic said to have been taken from the Crown of Thorns thrust upon Christ before the crucifixion. The 'Miracle of the Holy Thorn' made a very strong impression on Pascal. He interpreted it as a sign of divine approval of the Jansenist cause and began some sustained reflexion on the nature of miracles and their role in the understanding and confirmation of the Christian religion. It can be argued that his ultimate apologia for Christianity was rooted in this experience and broadened out from it. Eventually he lectured at Port-Royal on the plan of this apologia, probably in the spring of 1658, and in the autumn of the same year he worked on the classification of his notes which we know as the *Pensées*. Early in 1659 he became seriously ill again and had to give up all intellectual activity for more than a year. Late in 1660 we find him renewing his contacts with the Roannez family and with Méré and Mitton among others. It was around this time too that he wrote his *Trois Discours sur la condition des grands* which contain some telling comments on social rank and social responsibility based on his distinction between 'social' and 'natural' preeminence, between 'grandeurs d'établissement' and 'grandeurs naturelles'.

Pascal's last main involvement in the affairs of Port-Royal occurred in 1661 when the nuns were required by the Assembly of the Clergy and a decree of the Conseil d'Etat to sign a formulary condemning 'de cœur et de bouche' the five heretical propositions attributed to the *Augustinus* of Jansenius and asserting that Jansenius had misinterpreted the doctrine of Saint Augustine. The struggles of conscience which this demand made upon the nuns, and the unavailing search for an acceptable compromise, caused much suffering among them. And while several leading Jansenists were increasingly in favour of capitulation by the nuns, Pascal remained intransigent as his *Ecrit sur la signature du Formulaire* testifies.

These final years of Pascal's life were marked by considerable personal austerity and the performance of charitable works among the poor. Among other acts, he received a family of paupers into his own home. His health deteriorated again and he eventually died on 19 August 1662 at the age of thirty-nine. Eight years after his death, in 1670, the *Pensées* were published for the first time.

*   *   *   *   *

Initially the *Pensées* do not make easy reading. When looked at for the first time they present a very confusing jumble of unfinished bits and pieces rendered more difficult by a large number of classical and biblical quotations and allusions. Some are long, some are very short, and many are expressed in a condensed, elliptical manner. Again, different editors have put them in different sequences so that the individual fragments are given different numbers according to the system adopted by a particular editor. In fact, the *Pensées* involve us in a textual problem, as well as a problem of interpretation. It is therefore necessary to unravel the textual complications briefly here before going on, in the next chapter, to an explanation of Pascal's method of argument and apologetic approach.

By a piece of great good fortune we possess the manuscript originals, mostly in Pascal's own hand, of a high proportion of what are now known as the *Pensées*. The papers which Pascal left at his death, as notes for an 'Apologie de la religion chrétienne', fall into three groups. The first consists of twenty-eight *liasses* or collections of written sheets (of different sizes) originally threaded loosely together and each *liasse* provided with a general title. This group of papers is obviously the outcome of Pascal's effort to classify his notes and put them in an order for the purposes of his argument. One *liasse* remains blank apart from its title, 'La Nature est corrompue'. In modern arrangements of the *Pensées* essentially based on the work of Louis Lafuma, this group of *liasses* constitutes the first section and is numbered 1-27 with a 15 and 15b included, the latter being the blank *liasse*.

The second group of papers, containing about twice as many sheets as the first, was arranged in thirty-four roughly identifiable units. Unlike the first group, however, these had never been threaded together in *liasses* nor had they been given general titles, apart from one unit entitled 'Miscellanea'. These papers, which may or may not have been classified by Pascal himself, form section 2 of the Lafuma edition of the *Pensées*. They are followed in this edition by section 3 which consists of a separate collection of fragments on the subject of miracles. These probably constitute the original kernel of Pascal's apologia.

The third group of papers consists of varied pieces which I referred to earlier as an addendum to the *Pensées* since by no means all of them were originally destined to form part of the apologia. They appear as section 4 in the Lafuma arrangement and include such documents as the 'Mémorial', the 'Mystère de Jésus', and various fragments from other sources.

The subsequent story of the first two groups above — the titled *liasses* and the untitled units or *séries* (as Lafuma calls them) — is an interesting one. At the end of the seventeenth century they passed into the hands of Pascal's nephew, abbé Louis Périer, who had the originals pasted onto larger sheets and bound together to form an album. Where Pascal had written on both sides of a sheet of paper a rectangle of suitable size was cut in the album sheet so that both sides could be read. It is this pasting of the originals into an album which probably ensured the survival of the manuscript. The spine bears the title *Original des Pensées de Pascal* and the album is also referred to as the *Recueil original*.

While the *Original* ensured the survival of the manuscripts, it treated their order in a somewhat cavalier fashion. Also, individual sheets were cut up and separated so as to fit into blanks in the album, while other sheets were trimmed and clipped. This means that Pascal's initial classification would have been partly lost had it not been that several copies of the original manuscripts, in their original order, were made shortly after Pascal's death. Two of these, generally known as *La Copie* and *La Seconde Copie*, have been preserved and, like the *Recueil original*, are deposited in the Bibliothèque Nationale in Paris. The two copies are alike in their transcription of the *liasses*, but the *séries* are put in different sequences.

The other documents which are important for an understanding of Pascal's purpose in the *Pensées* should be mentioned. These are the two tables of contents, covering the first group of twenty-eight *liasses*, which accompany each of the two copies and are virtually identical. Although not in Pascal's hand, Mesnard has argued persuasively that they reproduce a document originally drawn up by Pascal himself.[1] It is noticeable that both tables have two columns of contents and this seems deliberate. The *liasses* listed in the left-hand column have to do predominantly with human experience and those in the right-hand one with divine revelation through Scripture. It would be a mistake, however, to interpret the two columns as two quite separate levels of argument. Rather, they should be seen as part of a single, developing line of reasoning which moves logically from an analysis of man (left-hand column) to knowledge of God (right-hand column).

The various documents described above have been treated very differently, and often ignored totally, in the large number of editions of the *Pensées* produced in the last three centuries. The first edition, which really ignored Pascal's apologetic strategy, was published in 1670 by a committee of editors grouped around Port-Royal. Apart from members of the Périer family, the editors included such Jansenists or Jansenist sympathizers as the Duc de Roannez, Filleau de la Chaise, Arnauld, Nicole and possibly Mme de Sablé. There was an interesting preface by Pascal's eldest nephew, Etienne Périer, which made it clear that the editors had decided not to attempt to reproduce Pascal's intended argument but to group the most complete

[1] Jean Mesnard, *Les Pensées de Pascal*, pp. 26-28.

passages around themes while ignoring those that were manifestly incomplete or contained any suggestion of unorthodoxy. Prudence was certainly required, even though the 'Peace of the Church' had brought a relative, if temporary, truce in the Jansenist controversy and made publication that much easier. So what this first edition mainly provided was a collection of Pascal's most fully expressed thoughts on religion and a variety of other topics.

The Port-Royal edition proved to be the model for succeeding presentations of the *Pensées* for more than a century. It is surprisingly late in the eighteenth century that a new classification and some new material appeared in the edition by the *philosophe* Condorcet published in 1776. Condorcet introduced much of the spirit of Enlightenment rationalism into his preface and the notes — mostly taken from Voltaire's highly critical *Remarques sur les Pensées de Pascal* — dissented strongly from many of Pascal's ideas. The other main eighteenth-century edition, published by abbé Bossut in 1779, was conceived in a similar spirit. Bossut made a distinction between 'philosophical' and 'religious' thoughts which enjoyed acceptance for many years and is still argued for by some present-day commentators.

The next important change came as a result of the intervention of Victor Cousin. In a report to the Académie Française of 1842, Cousin argued that a completely new edition of the *Pensées* was necessary, and in particular one that would go back to the manuscript sources provided by the *Recueil original* rather than to the very incomplete and partial Port-Royal edition. As a result this report was acted upon by P. Faugère who produced a two-volume edition of the *Pensées, fragments et lettres de Pascal* in 1844, based on the *Original* and containing an illuminating commentary and notes. It is of particular interest that Faugère attempted to arrange the text in accordance with Pascal's own apologetic intentions by taking as his guide Pascal's reference to his plan in the *Pensées*:

(1) Partie. Misère de l'homme sans Dieu.
(2) Partie. Félicité de l'homme avec Dieu.
        autrement

(1) Part. Que la nature est corrompue, par la nature même.
(2) Partie. Qu'il y a un Réparateur, par l'Ecriture.

                                                    (L.6, B.60)

The weakness of Faugère's method, of course, is that *he* chose
which fragments should go in which order and appears to have
been quite unaware of the classification of at least a third of the
material attributed to Pascal himself and directly represented in
the two copies.

Other nineteenth-century editions with excellent notes and
commentary include one by E. Havet published in 1852 and
reissued in revised form in 1866 and 1881. At the end of the century there appeared the very successful editions of Léon
Brunschvicg which held a dominant position for the first fifty
years of this century. In 1897 Brunschvicg published Pascal's
Opuscules et pensées, the title of which was changed to *Pensées
et opuscules* in subsequent printings. This is probably still the
best-known edition of the *Pensées*. It was followed between 1904
and 1914 by the fourteen-volume edition of the complete works
edited by Brunschvicg and including a three-volume edition of
the *Pensées*. The distinction is often made between the two
Brunschvicg editions by referring to that of 1897 as Brunschvicg
Minor and that of 1904-14 as Brunschvicg Major. The classification of Pascal's thoughts is the same in both editions and we find
Brunschvicg rejecting Pascal's plan (or what was then believed
to be his plan) and reverting to the system of the Port-Royal edition of classifying fragments according to various themes. As a
result the separation between 'philosophical' and 'religious'
themes was again intensified, though Brunschvicg brought to
both his editions a scholarly apparatus in terms of notes and
comments from which generations of students of Pascal have
drawn immense benefit.

The switching of attention by editors of the *Pensées* from the
manuscript of the *Original* to the first copy — a move which has
dominated recent scholarship on the subject — was mainly
initiated by Zacharie Tourneur. In 1942 he produced a
palaeographic edition of the *Pensées* which deciphered Pascal's
text at a new level of accuracy. In his introduction he examined

closely both the *Recueil original* and the first copy, and he argued in favour of use of the latter for purposes of classification. The trail blazed by Tourneur was followed independently by Louis Lafuma. His first arrangement of 1948 was something of a compromise between the old and the new approaches, but in 1951 he ordered Pascal's material strictly according to the indications of the first copy. This is the arrangement which he also followed twelve years later in the deservedly popular one-volume *Œuvres complètes* published in 1963. This and the Brunschvicg Minor are the best known and most widely used editions. Bidding strongly for similar popularity is an edition by Philippe Sellier based on the second copy and first published in 1976. It has attracted considerable interest and admiration, but this is not the place to debate the different virtues of the first and second copies. Rather, we must now turn our attention from the history of the *Pensées* to their content.

3 The Apologetic Design

It is important to be clear that the *Pensées* are a major work of Christian apologetics. The term 'Christian apologetics' generally means the exposition and advocacy of the Christian religion. Traditionally, Christian apologists have argued that religious belief is more reasonable than unbelief, that Christianity gives a uniquely persuasive account of its own credentials among the world's religious systems, and that orthodox Christianity is the most reasonable form of religious belief. Historically, the name 'apologist' was first used of a number of second-century Christians (including Justin Martyr and Tertullian) who expounded, defended and advocated the Christian case to their non-Christian contemporaries among the educated classes in the Roman Empire. This took place at a period when Christianity was still struggling within the framework of the state for the right to existence and freedom from persecution.

The situation in seventeenth-century France was very different. Nevertheless, humanist optimism and rational scepticism had both been encouraged by the Renaissance and a large body of apologetic literature appeared, much of it in response to these developments. We have seen that Pascal appears to have begun thinking about writing a work of apologetics in 1657 and that his apologia had taken general shape by 1658. Inevitably the *Pensées* themselves, in their very incomplete and sometimes unordered form, remain at some distance from the apologia for which they provide the initial notes and jottings. This distinct gap between the document which we possess (the *Pensées*) and the unwritten work of which they are the source (the *apologia*) has made it possible for a number of commentators on the *Pensées* to ignore — consciously or unconsciously — the apologetic element altogether. There are those, for example, who concentrate exclusively on Pascal's philosophical and psychological ideas, regarding the religious, and particularly the biblical, *pensées* as so much outdated and expendable mumbo-jumbo. It has been common to focus attention on Pascal's 'tragic vision' of man and the human condition, thus presenting a Pascal who appears to have much in common with the darker twentieth-century manifestations of existentialism and absurdism.

Such an interpretation has become increasingly difficult to justify, at least without considerable qualification. This is partly because it so often attributes to Pascal ideas and sentiments which he expressed not to represent his own outlook but that of the *libertins* to whom his apology was addressed. Secondly, and more importantly, such an interpretation falls before the discovery of Pascal's own ordering of part of his material which makes a predominantly secular or exclusively philosophical reading impossible to justify. In short, there is no getting away from the fact that the *Pensées* are the basis for a work of Christian apologetics and that the philosophical and psychological elements cannot be divorced from their theological implications. The evidence on which to base any understanding of Pascal's apologetic approach is scattered in a variety of documents and some of these sources, many of them outside the *Pensées* themselves, need to be examined a little more closely.

A general indication of Pascal's basic approach to apologetics is to be found in the preface which he wrote, in 1651, to a work on the vacuum which remained unfinished and unpublished. His *Préface. Sur le Traité du vide* is significant here because of the distinction made between three modes of knowledge — authority, reason, the senses — and his emphasis on the fact that authority and reason must not be confused, and are certainly not interchangeable, in certain fields of knowledge. In keeping with the trend of the new scientific revolution, he insists that science must be the object of rational inquiry, not of dogmatic authority. But conversely, and in contrast to Descartes and certain other contemporaries, he holds that theology is one of a number of areas of knowledge where the authority of the written texts, rather than rational deduction, is the only proper and acceptable starting-point. He writes in a well-known passage:

L'éclaircissement de cette différence doit nous faire plain-
dre l'aveuglement de ceux qui apportent la seule autorité
pour preuve dans les matières physiques, au lieu du raisonnement ou des expériences, et nous donner de l'horreur
pour la malice des autres qui emploient le raisonnement
seul dans la théologie au lieu de l'autorité de l'Ecriture et
des Pères (L., p.231).

This is an early indication of the importance which Pascal was to
give to the authority of the Bible, and of Church Fathers such as
Augustine, in his apology. This does not exclude the making of a
reasonable case, based on biblical authority, but it does mean
that he interpreted the Bible in a manner far removed from later
textual criticism but very much in the spirit of the commentaries
associated with Port-Royal in general and Le Maître de Saci in
particular.

Another document which throws important light on Pascal's
apologetic strategy is Fontaine's account of the conversation (or
possibly a résumé of several conversations) which took place
between Pascal and his confessor and spiritual director, Le
Maître de Saci, at Port-Royal-des-Champs early in 1655. One is
struck — and indeed Le Maître de Saci was at first very un-
favourably impressed — by Pascal's claims that the works of
Epictetus and Montaigne had been his most constant reading.
He admires both writers and describes Epictetus as 'un des
philosophes du monde qui aient mieux connu les devoirs de
l'homme' (L.,p.292). He goes on to characterize the austere
stoical teaching of Epictetus: 'Ayez tous les jours devant les yeux
la mort et les maux qui semblent les plus insupportables et
jamais vous ne penserez rien de bas, et ne désirerez rien avec
excès' (L.,p.293). He praises the assertion by Epictetus that the
whole purpose of the individual should be to discover and obey
God's will. Nevertheless, immediately afterwards, he attacks
Epictetus for teaching that man possesses powers of intellect and
will enabling him to attain his own highest and godlike ideals
and to achieve moral perfection. This attitude is regarded by
Pascal as 'une superbe diabolique', an overwhelming pride totally
at variance with human reality. As regards Montaigne, Pascal

admires his questioning spirit and the way in which he uses his sceptical gifts 'pour prouver la vanité des opinions les plus reçues'. Montaigne is, in fact, in contrast to Epictetus, a total sceptic ('pur pyrrhonien') who nevertheless uses his scepticism in such a way that 'il combat avec une fermeté invincible les hérétiques de son temps, sur ce qu'ils s'assuraient de connaître seuls le véritable sens de l'Ecriture; et c'est de là encore qu'il foudroie plus rigoureusement l'impiété horrible de ceux qui osent assurer que Dieu n'est point' (L.,p.294). At this point Fontaine comments with what we can only hope is conscious humour: 'M. de Saci se croyant vivre dans un nouveau pays et entendre une nouvelle langue, il se disait en lui-même les paroles de Saint Augustin: "O Dieu de vérité! ceux qui savent ces subtilités de raisonnement vous sont-ils pour cela plus agréables?" ' However, Pascal goes on to criticize Montaigne as severely as he had Epictetus. What he finds pernicious in Montaigne's scepticism is that it leads to despair and a rejection of responsibility and values. In Pascal's view Montaigne's thought is fundamentally nihilistic, believing that 'l'ignorance et l'incuriosité sont deux doux oreillers pour une tête bien faite' (L.,p.296).

What Pascal does at this point is to emphasize the contrast, indeed the contradiction, between the excessive confidence of Stoicism and the enfeebling negativity of Pyrrhonism. The contrast, put into seventeenth-century terms, is one between the moral optimism of the *honnête homme* and the searching disbelief of the *libertin*, and both lead logically to unacceptably extreme positions. 'C'est donc de ces lumières imparfaites qu'il arrive que l'un, connaissant les devoirs de l'homme et ignorant son impuissance, se perd dans la présomption, et que l'autre, connaissant l'impuissance et non le devoir, il s'abat dans la lâcheté.' But Pascal also points out that these two positions are incompatible: '...ils ne peuvent subsister seuls à cause de leurs défauts, ni s'unir à cause de leurs oppositions, et ... ainsi ils se brisent et s'anéantissent pour faire place à la vérité de l'Evangile'. The last phrase here is particularly significant and brings us back to Pascal's apologetic strategy. As we shall see later, he planned for his apology and included in his *Pensées* an account of man which underlines both his greatness and his feebleness, thereby creating a similar and apparently insoluble contradiction — insoluble until one discovers the explanation uniquely offered by Christianity. The movement of the argument in the *Entretien avec M. de Saci*, as in the *Pensées*, is one from human contradiction to divine illumination. Only the insights and teachings of the Christian religion can rescue secular thoughts from inconsistency and self-destruction.

Two documents written by associates of Pascal generally confirm the pattern of argument so far suggested. These are Etienne Périer's preface to the Port-Royal edition of the *Pensées* and an account of the 1658 Port-Royal lecture written by Filleau de la Chaise. The Périer preface is the less satisfactory of these two documents, not least because of the excessive emphasis which it contains on the gap between the text of the *Pensées* and Pascal's apologetic design. Indeed Périer appears to make a knowledge of Pascal's ultimate purpose largely irrelevant to the *Pensées* when he writes: 'On verra parmi les fragments que l'on donne au public quelque chose de ce grand dessein de M. Pascal, mais on y en verra bien peu; et les choses mêmes que l'on y trouvera sont si imparfaites, si peu étendues et si peu digérées, qu'elles ne peuvent donner qu'une idée très grossière de la manière dont il avait envie de les traiter' (L.,p.497).

Although Etienne Périer does not relate the intended apologia and the actual *Pensées* in a way that would satisfy modern scholars, he does in fact give a succinct account in his preface of Pascal's apologetic design. This is mainly so because he summarizes the *Discours sur les Pensées de M. Pascal où l'on essaye de faire voir quel était son dessein* written by Jean Filleau de la Chaise and originally intended as a preface to the *Pensées*. It appears to be a secondhand account, produced seven or eight years after the event, of what Pascal said in his Port-Royal lecture. Nevertheless, it possesses the great virtue not only of giving a detailed account of Pascal's lecture but of relating various individual *pensées* to the complete scheme which Pascal outlined. Where Périer remains at the level of generalities, Filleau de la Chaise provides documentary detail. Furthermore, Filleau de la Chaise evaluates the persuasive quality of Pascal's argument and makes clear the distinction between Pascal's approach and that of more traditional apologetics based on natural theology: 'La vérité est qu'il ne faut pas tant penser à prouver Dieu qu'à le faire sentir'.[2] This is a direct response to Pascal's definition of faith as 'Dieu sensible au cœur, non à la raison' (L.424, B.278) and is consistent with the distinction made in the preface to the *Traité du vide* between the different kinds of demonstration appropriate respectively to scientific and religious truths. This is therefore a suitable point at which to look more closely at Pascal's epistemology or theory of knowledge as it affects his apologetic design.

In keeping with the teaching of Augustinianism, Pascal rejected the methods of natural theology. While he insisted on the need to present a reasonable case for Christianity, he denied that true knowledge of God could be achieved solely by human reason. For one thing, man's rational thinking is so radically different from the nature of deity that it cannot encompass it. The finite cannot comprehend the infinite: 'Nous connaissons donc l'existence et la nature du fini, parce que nous sommes finis et étendus comme lui ... Mais nous ne connaissons ni l'existence ni la nature de Dieu, parce qu'il n'a ni étendue ni bornes' (L.418, B.233). Furthermore, Pascal rejects rational 'proofs' of Christianity (e.g. those of Descartes) because they present us only with intellectual concepts, not existential realities, and thus they do not transform our lives as they should. Rational thought may lead to a belief in the intellectual idea of divinity, but such a belief remains intellectually vulnerable and fails to give personal knowledge of God. Pascal insists: '... je n'entreprendrai pas ici de prouver par des raisons naturelles, ou l'existence de Dieu, ou la Trinité, ou l'immortalité de l'âme, ni aucune des choses de cette nature', and he adds: 'Quand un homme serait persuadé que les proportions des nombres sont des vérités immatérielles, éternelles et dépendantes d'une première vérité en qui elles subsistent, et qu'on appelle Dieu, je ne le trouverais pas beaucoup avancé pour son salut' (L.449, B.556).

If Pascal rejects in this way the *a priori* arguments of apologetics based on natural theology, he also rejects *a*

[2]Filleau de la Chaise, *Discours sur les Pensées de M. Pascal* (ed. V. Giraud), Paris, Bossard, 1922, p. 35.

posteriori reasoning. In particular, he opposes the traditional 'argument from design' or deduction of God's existence from what is claimed to be pattern and purpose in nature — what he calls 'prouver la divinité par les ouvrages de la nature' (L.781, B.242). He makes three main points. First, the argument from design is not an effective means of convincing unbelievers since the predisposition to see or fail to see a divine plan in nature depends on our prior religious attitude. We simply find what we already believe exists, or fail to find that in which we have no prior belief. So the argument appeals to subjectivity and has no objectively demonstrable qualities. Second, Pascal dismisses this argument because it has no scriptural authority: 'C'est une chose admirable que jamais auteur canonique ne s'est servi de la nature pour prouver Dieu' (L.463, B.243). The *deus absconditus* or 'hidden God' of Jansenism and Augustinianism reveals Himself much less readily and less often than would the God of nature posited by the argument from design. Pascal does not deny that God does reveal Himself by other means to the elect and that they consequently see the works of nature as His handiwork. But it is God who reveals the truth concerning nature, not nature which reveals the existence of God. Third, Pascal is convinced that even if the arguement from design could, *per impossibile*, prove the existence of God, it would not prove the existence of the specifically Christian God. At best, it would justify some vague form of transcendentalism or rational deism.

Pascal's rejection of these various forms of rationalistic apologetics is in keeping with his distinction, in the preface to the *Traité du vide*, between the different kinds of demonstration appropriate to scientific and religious truths respectively. Nevertheless, although the preface associated religious conviction with authority, he certainly does not require unquestioning submission to received dogma on the part of his readers. His problem, having renounced purely rational reasoning, is to show on what grounds and in what way the particular form of knowledge called belief can be made acceptable, indeed reasonable, and thus provide the vital link between the human dilemma which he describes and the scriptural solution which he proposes.

Behind Pascal's apologetic position lies the fundamental

distinction which he makes in the *Pensées* between the so-called 'three orders' and which is the outcome of his investigation and reflexion in the spheres of social and political questions, mathematical and scientific matters, and philosophy and religion. The three orders of experience which he lists are presented in somewhat different terminology in different fragments, but the basic distinctions are clear enough and were touched on in various earlier apologetic writings including those of Augustine and of Pascal's near-contemporary Bérulle. The three orders are the physical, the intellectual and the spiritual — *chair*, *esprit*, *charité* — and individuals tend to belong to one or other category. There are those whose talents are mainly in the practical, material order of things, those whose gifts are predominantly intellectual, and those whose instincts are deeply spiritual. In the fragment which sets out the three orders most clearly and fully (L.308, B.793) Pascal insists on the radical discontinuity between them. It is clear that he places them in ascending rank, starting with the physical or material and ending, at the highest point, with the spiritual. Having stated that each order is separated from the others by infinite distance, he continues:

> La grandeur des gens d'esprit est invisible aux rois, aux riches, aux capitaines, à tous ces grands de chair.

> La grandeur de la sagesse, qui n'est nulle sinon de Dieu, est invisible aux charnels et aux gens d'esprit. Ce sont trois ordres différents, de genre.

The conclusion to be drawn from these categories — one which is particularly relevant to apologetics — is that such different orders of experience and achievement require different modes of inquiry and methods of demonstration. Apologetics has to do above all with the intellectual and spiritual orders, and here Pascal draws a sharp distinction between the different types of understanding which they demand: 'Le cœur a son ordre, l'esprit a le sien qui est par principe et démonstration. Le cœur en a un autre. On ne prouve pas qu'on doit être aimé en exposant d'ordre les causes de l'amour; cela serait ridicule' (L.298, B.283). In other words, intellectual knowledge and intuitive understanding are profoundly different in nature and require very different forms of demonstration. It is also clear that Pascal's distinction between the *esprit de géométrie* and the *esprit de finesse*, mentioned in the previous chapter, is relevant here. The *esprit de géométrie* (the rational, deductive mind) is essential in the intellectual order but inappropriate in the spiritual or intuitive. Conversely, the *esprit de finesse* (the intuitive mind or *le cœur*) is appropriate to the spiritual order but inadequate at the purely intellectual level.

It is to the 'order of the heart' above all that Pascal directs his apology. The term 'heart' or 'cœur' can easily mislead, however, and Pascal has been accused of mindless sentimentality because of his well-known statement that 'le cœur a ses raisons que la raison ne connaît point' (L.423, B.277). Similarly, he has been held to have sacrificed reason and renounced intelligent belief when he wrote: 'C'est le cœur qui sent Dieu et non la raison' (L.424, B.278). But in fact Pascal remained an outstanding intellectual to the end of his life and these accusations are based on a misunderstanding of his use of the term 'cœur'. He uses it in at least three different senses, one of which is intimately connected with his apologetic design.

In psychological contexts Pascal uses 'cœur' in the familiar sense of the emotional or sentimental element in our nature. In more philosophical circumstances he employs the term to describe our innate apprehension of certain general principles: 'Le cœur sent qu'il y a trois dimensions dans l'espace et que les nombres sont infinis, et la raison démontre ensuite qu'il n'y a point deux nombres carrés dont l'un soit double de l'autre. Les principes se sentent, les propositions se concluent et le tout avec certitude quoique par différentes voies' (L.110, B.282). It is clear that the word 'cœur' here has nothing to do with emotionalism or sentimentality. But Pascal also uses it to convey something like the focal point in the personality where intelligence, feeling and will come together in such a way that they provide knowledge which is direct and intuitive but which could not have been attained by exclusively rational means. The psalmist seems to be referring to the same focal point of the personality as the instrument of spiritual knowledge when he writes (in what was Pascal's favourite psalm): 'With my whole heart have I sought thee' (Psalm 119.10). What is involved is an act of will, emotion and intelligence. It is an act in which belief precedes and facilitates knowledge. The design of Pascal's apologia is therefore an unusual and intriguing one. Using what he holds to be eminently reasonable arguments, he attempts to arouse in his readers a response to Christianity which does not insist on rational demonstration as a prelude to belief but which adopts a set of beliefs that are eventually confirmed by subsequent argument. He paints a portrait of man which can be interpreted as giving reasonable grounds for belief and he then authenticates this belief by an exposition of the authority of Scripture, an appeal to the experience of regular worship ('la coutume'), etc. His apologetic design is one which is calculated to bring an antecedent belief to consciousness of its own historical and spiritual justification. One is reminded of the famous and striking statement from St Anselm's *Proslogion*: 'For I do not seek to understand in order that I may believe, but I believe in order that I may understand'. Pascal was keenly aware that God's existence could neither be proved nor disproved by purely rational means (L.809, B.230) and he therefore had to show that belief in the Christian God was reasonable — reasonable in the light of man's contradictory nature and reasonable in the light of biblical teaching. Indeed, there is no question of Pascal regarding Christianity at large as anything but reasonable and certain, but he accepted that this conviction could not be reached by the wholly rational methods of the philosophers. He writes: 'La religion chrétienne qui seule a la raison n'admet point pour ses vrais enfants ceux qui croient sans inspiration. Ce n'est pas qu'elle exclue la raison et la coutume, au contraire; mais il faut ouvrir son esprit aux preuves, s'y confirmer par la coutume, mais s'offrir par les humiliations aux inspirations, qui seules peuvent faire le vrai et salutaire effet' (L.808, B.245). The design of Pascal's apologia, reasonably enough, is theological rather than philosophical. The theory of the three orders, let alone the teaching of the Bible, requires that it should be so.

The outline of Pascal's apology described by Périer and Filleau de la Chaise is not only further explained by certain passages in the *Pensées* but confirmed in its design by a lengthy fragment headed 'A.P.R.' (L.149, B.430). These letters are taken to stand for 'A Port-Royal' and the fragment appears to have been written by Pascal with his Port-Royal lecture in mind. 'A.P.R.' confirms the strategy by which Pascal reveals the essential contradictoriness of human nature and then shows how this contradictoriness is uniquely explained by Christianity: 'Les grandeurs et les misères de l'homme sont tellement visibles qu'il faut nécessairement que la véritable religion enseigne et ... nous rende raison de ces étonnantes contrariétés'. Given this type of argument, one can say that Pascal's apology is explanatory and man-based in character. It interprets Christianity as a totally convincing explanation of the nature of man and is strongly scriptural. But 'A.P.R.' also makes it clear that this is what is called a soteriological apologia. That is to say, it claims not only to explain man by means of Christian teaching, but to give him the possibility of total salvation. It both sets out 'la cause de ces faiblesses' of which man is a victim, and offers 'les remèdes qui les peuvent guérir'. In fact, 'Dieu a voulu racheter les hommes et ouvrir le salut à ceux qui le chercheraient'. Consequently, far from making a purely intellectual case for Christianity and God's existence, Pascal equates genuine knowledge of God, arrived at through faith and 'le cœur', with eternal salvation.

It is clear that Pascal did not sketch out his arguments in the *Pensées* without taking account of other and earlier apologetic writings. For example, he makes explicit reference to Martini's *Pugio fidei adversus Mauros et Judeos* (1276-78) which he read in the 1651 Voisin edition (L.277, 483, B.635, 726). He similarly refers to Grotius's *De veritate religionis christianae* of 1627 (L.498, B.715) and the *Pensées* show evidence of significant further borrowing from this source. From Grotius he derived some of his objections to Mohammedanism and from Martini he gleaned useful information on the Jewish religion and biblical prophecy. But both these works belong to the predominantly scholarly and historical apologetic tradition which, while it clearly had a distinctive role to play in Pascal's intended apology, was far removed from a set of arguments aimed at *libertin* apathy such as Pascal had in mind. Also, neither work was much concerned with an analysis of man's nature and metaphysical condition — and both made rather dull reading.

A more spiritual presentation, with much greater emphasis on man's nature, is to be found in some of the apologetic works belonging to the Augustinian tradition, and particularly the *De vera religione* of Augustine himself. This late fourth-century work had been translated by Arnauld in 1647 and there was a further edition in 1656. It seems certain that Pascal read it — with its demonstration that the Christian religion can alone provide a satisfactory explanation of man's contradictory and enigmatic nature, and its soteriological emphasis on the remedies which Christianity uniquely provides for man's misery. It seems equally certain that Pascal read both Montaigne's translation and his defence of Raymond Sebonde's *Theologia naturalis* of 1484. Sebonde begins from the position that nothing created can be closer to man than man himself and proceeds to argue that religion must be explained by the study of man. He presents an Augustinian account of man's fallen state and goes on to assert that only Christianity can save him, that the Christian God is a God of salvation. Here again we are reminded of the humane and soteriological character of Pascal's own apologetic design. Indeed, Sebonde outlines what was to be Pascal's design when he summarizes his own thought: 'L'homme se doit toujours avoir devant les yeux, à cette heure originellement homme, à cette heure homme perdu, à cette heure homme remis'. This is the general position adopted in the seventeenth century by such predecessors of Pascal as Bérulle and his fellow Oratorian Senault. The latter's *L'Homme criminel* and *L'Homme racheté* were published in 1644 and 1646 respectively. These Augustinian apologists never adopted the extreme Jansenist position of denying all goodness in man and in this respect Pascal also remains at one remove from the most severe Jansenism. The *Pensées* repeatedly remind us of man's dual nature, of good and bad, and Pascal says quite clearly of man: '... il y a en lui une nature capable de bien' (L.119, B.423).

It will be clear from what has been said here that many features of Pascal's apologia can be found, in one form or another, in the apologetic literature mainly available at this period. At the same time, Pascal continues to be the best known and most widely read of seventeenth-century apologists. This is so even in those cases where his apologetic intention is not always fully understood or properly acknowledged. There are a number of possible reasons for this. It could be argued, for instance, that his achievements in so many fields — scientific and mathematical as well as psychological and religious — give him special status. He is one of the intellectual giants of the period. It has also been suggested that the notes and fragments forming the *Pensées*, precisely because they lack final form and shape, possess an enduring attractiveness and continue to permit a freedom of interpretation which a finished and tightly argued discursive work would not allow. One might also suggest that the more open and loose the *Pensées* remain, the more they avoid a logical contradiction between the expression of Pascal's argument and the type of response, dependent on will and belief, which he seeks to create. His method of persuasion remains subtle and complex. But perhaps Pascal stands out most clearly from his fellow apologists because of the skill with which he deploys arguments already used by others, the way in which he gives such arguments new sharpness and significance, and more generally because of his outstanding literary gifts.

The first of these points is put by Pascal himself with characteristic verve and by typical recourse to an unexpected image 'Qu'on ne dise pas que je n'ai rien dit de nouveau, la disposition des matières est nouvelle. Quand on joue à la paume c'est une même balle dont joue l'un et l'autre, mais l'un la place mieux' (L.696, B.22). It seems appropriate here to look briefly at an instance of this skilful use of familiar material. An example would be the famous 'wager argument' ('le pari') used in the *Pensées* (L.418, B.233). Pascal suggests first of all that the gambling in which his *libertin* friends indulge is not, strictly speaking, irrational: 'Tout joueur hasarde avec certitude pour gagner avec incertitude; et néanmoins il hasarde certainement le fini pour gagner incertainement le fini, sans pécher contre la raison'. By the same token, if one were to 'wager' on God's existence, it would not be irrational to argue as follows: if I assume that God exists and he does not, I lose very little; if he does exist and I have assumed this, my gain now and in the world to come is immense. If I make the opposite assumption, namely that God does not exist, and in fact he does not, again I lose very little; if he does exist, however, then my assumption of his non-existence was totally wrong and my loss now and in the world to come is immense. The two really striking possibilities here are thus infinite gain or infinite loss. Neither can be ensured in advance, but the logical choice is to wager on God's existence.

It is obvious that we are not dealing here with a proof or *demonstration* of God's existence. At most it is a *device* to seek to break down the apathy of the *libertin* and to speak to him in his own language. But what is of interest in the present context is the way in which Pascal alters what was a fairly widely used argument. For one thing, the wager argument was mostly applied to the question of the immortality of the soul. It had been used in this way, with varying degrees of rigour, by such different seventeenth-century apologists as Sirmond, Caussin, Richeôme, Silhon, Yves de Paris, etc. So Pascal is different in so far as he relates the argument to God's existence. It is true that one or two writers — mainly Mersenne in 1623 — had used it to prove God's existence. Here again Pascal is distinctive. He certainly does not treat it as a proof, and in any case he gives to the argument a unique mathematical flavour arising from his own work on the mathematics of probability. Above all, his use of the wager is distinctive because he exploits it not to appeal primarily to the reader's self-interest but in order to reveal within it the presence of a certain necessity: 'Oui, mais il faut parier. Cela n'est pas volontaire, vous êtes embarqués'. According to Pascal, then, we are compelled to make the choice implied in the wager argument. The argument is structured in such a way that to abstain from the choice offered is tantamount to rejecting God. Whatever way we look at it we are committed — and committed by the same argument that Sartre was to use in a secular context three centuries later. This idea that neutrality is impossible in certain situtions is repeated in other parts of the

Pensées. On the subject of original sin, for example, Pascal writes in the same spirit: '... il faut que chacun prenne parti, et se range nécessairement ou au dogmatisme ou au pyrrhonisme. Car qui pensera demeurer neutre sera pyrrhonien par excellence' (L.131, B.434). It is clearly important to try to convince the *libertin* that apathy itself is a form of commitment and not of neutrality.

There is evidence that Pascal paid a good deal of attention to the question of communication and persuasion. His gifts in this direction were admired by many of his contemporaries. There is little doubt, therefore, that his ability to argue persuasively and his literary skill are among the most important features that have ensured the survival of the *Pensées* and the case for belief which they make. It is worth repeating too, that he wrote as a layman, not as a trained theologian or as a man in religious orders. The result is that he was that much better fitted to appeal to a wide and mainly secular readership. Here again he differed from virtually all the apologists of his own age.

We saw in the previous chapter that Pascal wrote an *Art de persuader*, probably late in 1655 and before he embarked on the polemics of his *Lettres provinciales*. Part of the interest of *De l'art de persuader* is the awareness which it shows of the way that people arrive at their most firmly held opinions. They do so, according to Pascal, by exercising either the understanding or the will. The understanding is the more powerful source of conviction, but the will is the more common, so that '... tout ce qu'il y a d'hommes sont presque toujours emportés à croire non pas par la preuve, mais par l'agrément' (L., p.355). Put more familiarly, Pascal is saying that people believe what they want to believe in most instances. He is aware that this makes it particularly difficult to persuade the *libertin* to accept a Christian belief which he finds basically unattractive. The Christian apologist, indeed, is faced with the problem that, in a perverse kind of way, men come to basically emotional conclusions about things which require a rational response yet demand that spiritual truths should satisfy the most stringent rational criteria. Part of Pascal's purpose is to reverse this situation and persuade his readers that the *esprit de géométrie* must be exercised in the sphere of natural science and the *esprit de finesse* in the sphere of religion. Indeed it would be hard to deny that this is his main persuasive purpose. He must somehow prevail upon the *libertin* to face unpalatable truths and accept them by an act of will. And yet this is something which he cannot fully accomplish as a human being. Pascal recognizes that he himself cannot bring his readers to faith in the fullest sense of the word. Only God can do this: 'Dieu seul peut mettre [les vérités divines] dans l'âme, et par la manière qui lui plaît' (L., p.355). It follows that Pascal must see his apologia as an instrument which God may or may not use; a channel through which God may decide to communicate His grace to men. And so however much the *Pensées* are designed to convince, they can only put men into the right attitude of mind and spirit to receive grace. They cannot, as an intellectual and literary structure, convey true grace directly.

Nevertheless, it is clear that matters of verbal expression have a role to play in Pascal's overall strategy, even if their role cannot be a determining one. We can hardly read the *Pensées* without being impressed by their often striking formulation. There is, moreover, something close to a paradox in the fact that an unfinished work — a collection of notes and some more carefully reworked fragments — should possess such outstanding literary qualities. More deliberately constructed and carefully expressed passages include some comments on imagination and prejudice (L.44, B.82), a fairly detailed survey of scepticism (L.131, B.434), or a lengthy comparison between the principles of free thought and those of Christian apologetics (L.427, B.194). But Pascal also appears to have possessed the relatively rare gift of being able to create epigrams and produce memorable images in an almost spontaneous manner. A scrutiny of his manuscripts provides evidence of the speed with which he sought to get some of his ideas down on paper. But the evidence also suggests that at times this very haste, far from formulating his thought loosely, concentrated his mind in such a way that he found particularly appropriate images and phrases by what appears to have been an impressive form of artistic instinct.

In these more spontaneous passages, and also in the more

'finished' ones, Pascal wrote to be understood by the widest
possible audience. In an effort to stir a positive response in his
readers, he avoided both excessive literary embellishment and
the jargon of theology and philosophy. He adopted an
essentially universal language, wrote what for his
contemporaries was modern prose, and turned his back on the
linguistic pedantry of grammarians and *précieux* on the one
hand, and of logicians and Sorbonne doctors on the other.
Universality (in keeping with his subject-matter) and naturalness
(in keeping with his aesthetic ideals) combined to form the style
of the *honnête homme* which Pascal admired and advocated. He
writes: 'Quand on voit le style naturel on est tout étonné et ravi,
car on s'attendait de voir un auteur et on trouve un homme'
(L.675, B.29). In producing the natural, personal prose of the
Pensées he uses the resources of style at his command. But he
does so for essentially utilitarian purposes — to make his
arguments more telling and not to trick out the expression of his
ideas with decorative effects devoid of organic function.

At a general level, critics have commented on certain
persistent characteristics of Pascal's choice of vocabulary and
on his feeling for the *mot juste*. For example, when writing of
man's cosmic situation, he often uses the vocabulary of
mathematical thought as when he describes the universe as 'une
sphère infinie dont le centre est partout, la circonférence nulle
part' (L.199, B.72), or when he defines man within this universe
as 'un néant à l'égard de l'infini, un tout à l'égard du néant, un
milieu entre rien et tout, infiniment éloigné de comprendre les
extrêmes ...' On the other hand, he also uses a contrasting
vocabulary of instability, fragility or eternal motion when
describing man's subjective experience of his human condition.
The lengthy fragment from which the 'mathematical' phrases
above have been quoted contains a notable example: 'Nous
voguons sur un milieu vaste, toujours incertains et flottants,
poussés d'un bout vers l'autre; quelque terme où nous pensions
nous attacher et nous affermir, il branle, et nous quitte, et si
nous le suivons il échappe à nos prises, nous glisse et fuit d'une
fuite éternelle; rien ne s'arrête pour nous'. This repeated pattern
of 'hard' and 'soft' words and images gives to Pascal's prose in

the *Pensées* a very distinctive character. It makes for that clarity
and precision, yet shot through with an element of imaginative
disquiet, which we associate with what is best in classical art and
notably embodied, for instance, in the famous 'roseau pensant'
image (L.200, B.347).

The prose used in the *Pensées* is striking because of its clear,
concise and often concrete nature. The clarity and conciseness
vary from the straightforward simplicity of 'Pensée fait la
grandeur de l'homme' (L.759, B.346) to the much more complex
structure of the fragment beginning: 'Il est juste que ce qui est
juste soit suivi' (L.103, B.298). While this is a feature shared by
much aphoristic writing of the period, Pascal stands out because
of his frequent preference for concrete rather than abstract
formulations. Not the least important part of his skill as a writer
is his awareness of those different occasions when either
concrete or abstract expressions are required. As he puts it in the
Pensées: 'Il y a des lieux où il faut appeler Paris, Paris, et
d'autres où il la faut appeler capitale du royaume' (L.509, B.49).

A typical example of Pascal's use of a concrete image to
convey an abstract idea is provided by the strongly visual
reference to two urchins quarrelling over the ownership of a dog
or a place in the sun: 'Mien, tien. Ce chien est à moi, disaient ces
pauvres enfants. C'est là ma place au soleil. Voilà le
commencement et l'image de l'usurpation de toute la terre'
(L.64, B.295). Here, of course, the abstract reference of the
concrete image is spelled out clearly by Pascal himself. On other
occasions he leaves concrete images to make their impact
without explicit commentary: 'On croit toucher des orgues
ordinaires en touchant l'homme. Ce sont des orgues à la vérité,
mais bizarres, changeantes, variables. (*Ceux qui ne savent
toucher que les ordinaires*) ne seraient pas d'accord sur celles-là.
Il faut savoir où sont les (touches)' (L.55, B.111). Perhaps the
most conclusive evidence of Pascal's frequent preference for the
concrete rather than the abstract is to be found in a study of his
manuscript corrections. We know from these corrections that he
altered 'aveugler' to 'crever les yeux' (L.44, B.82),
'imaginations' to 'vains fantômes' (L.131, B.434), 'ignorance'
to 'ténèbres' (L.149, B.430), etc. But he also appears to have

found more immediately, and without prior correction, such memorable expressions as 'le nœud de notre condition' (L.131, B.434) or 'La guerre intestine de l'homme' (L.621, B.412).

In addition to an often original and memorable use of images, Pascal's prose is noteworthy for the way in which he controls and varies his phrasing within sentences and his sentences in relation to one another. He writes with a finely judged sense of rhythm and balance. These comments on man's relationship with God are typical:

> La connaissance de Dieu sans celle de sa misère fait l'orgueil.
> La connaissance de sa misère sans celle de Dieu fait le désespoir.
> La connaissance de J.-C. fait le milieu parce que nous y trouvons, et Dieu et notre misère. (L.192, B.527)

The balance between the first two lines here, involving reversal and contrast, is characteristic of Pascal's frequent use of symmetry. But the last two lines add something further. They intensify the symmetry by indicating a point of balance ('le milieu') which also suggests a resolution of the previous contrasts ('orgueil/désespoir', 'connaissance de Dieu/ connaissance de sa misère'). The structure here resembles that of the dialectic (thesis/antithesis/synthesis) and it is wholly in keeping with Pascal's apologia since his purpose is to resolve the contrasting elements of man's nature through the 'synthesis' offered by Christian teaching. In other words, Pascal's dialectical strategy is often expressed both by the words which he actually uses and by their disposition in a series of sentences:

> S'il se vante je l'abaisse.
> S'il s'abaisse je le vante.
> Et le contredis toujours.
> Jusqu'à ce qu'il comprenne
> Qu'il est un monstre incompréhensible. (L.130, B.420)

It is hardly necessary to point out here that the last two lines

('...qu'il *comprenne* qu'il est ... *incompréhensible*') contain an example of Pascal's tendency to introduce a play on words. Here it is a question of mild paradox — understanding that one cannot be understood –- while in an example given earlier the play was with two different meanings of the same word: 'Il est juste que ce qui est juste soit suivi'.

Finally, it is worth pointing out that there are moments of very complex stylization in the *Pensées* — moments of high drama, as it were, in which Pascal brings all his stylistic resources to bear in an attempt to rouse his reader's attention and convince his mind. Such moments naturally occur in the more carefully reworked passages. One of the famous portraits of man, for example, brings together exclamations, assertions, rhetorical questions, accumulated nouns and sharply balanced contrasts: 'Quelle chimère est-ce donc que l'homme? quelle nouveauté, quel monstre, quel chaos, quel sujet de contradictions, quel prodige? Juge de toutes choses, imbécile ver de terre, dépositaire du vrai, cloaque d'incertitude et d'erreur, gloire et rebut de l'univers' (L.131, B.434). Here Pascal pulls out all those special organ stops — 'bizarres, changeantes, variables' — to which he referred in L.55, B.111. Yet even here it is his apologetic purpose rather than his literary virtuosity which is foremost in his mind. However apparently obtrusive his style, his intention remains moral and psychological rather than artistic. He had no interest in literary achievement purely for its own sake. His rhetoric is rooted in psychology rather than aesthetics.

4 The Human Dilemma

We have seen that it was an essential part of Pascal's apologetic design to show that the irreconcilable contrasts which characterize the human condition can only be explained by the Christian account of man and the world. This has two important consequences. It means that the argument implied in the *Pensées* does not begin with dogmatic and doctrinal religious assertions. On the contrary, it moves from a practical study of man to the subsequent religious implications which Pascal sees in it. The movement is one from secular problem to religious solution. It also means that a significant proportion of the *Pensées* is taken up with a close analysis of human experience. Indeed, Pascal regarded the study of human behaviour as being of the utmost importance. For him, 'the proper study of mankind is man', and he asserts: '... la science des mœurs me consolera toujours de l'ignorance des sciences extérieures' (L.23, B.67. See also L.687, B.144). And so the analysis which he makes is both comprehensive and dramatic, covering four aspects of man's nature: the psychological (the individual's own nature); the social (the individual and others); the metaphysical (the individual and the universe); the theological (the individual and the Christian message). And all these aspects are closely related and integrated despite the fragmentary surface appearance of the *Pensées*.

The first of these aspects, the moral/psychological, shows the contradictory nature of man in the most obvious and straightforward way. The contrast between man's moral weaknesses and moral strengths is implied by Pascal's repeated *misère/grandeur* antithesis. As regards his weaknesses, man is fickle, restless and lacks stability. This inconstancy is such that the same spectacle can make us laugh or cry, depending on our mood (L.54, B.112) and human reactions are often impossible to predict. This wayward, arbitrary element in much human behaviour is explained by the fact that man is a constant victim of what Pascal terms the 'puissances trompeuses', particularly various forms of emotion and imagination. In general terms he sees the emotional basis underlying so many ostensibly rational positions and concludes that 'tout notre raisonnement se réduit à céder au sentiment' (L.530, B.274). Subjectivity determines many of our supposedly objective conclusions. His observation of the way in which society conducts its affairs even moves him to conclude that 'l'affection ou la haine changent la justice de face' (L.44, B.82). But emotions that have little to do with self-interest may also undermine the conclusions of reason. A fearful imagination may do so, with the result that 'le plus grand philosophe du monde sur une planche plus large qu'il ne faut, s'il y a au-dessous un précipice, quoique sa raison le convainque de sa sûreté, son imagination prévaudra' (L.44, B.82). And so, although man is characterized above all by the gift of reason, and although thought makes him great, his reason is clearly limited and often subject to the powerful effect of his emotions and prejudices. Reason is therefore undermined by the corrupting effect of sense and emotion. But we saw in the previous chapter that Pascal also regarded it as limited in applicability. There are many areas of human experience and inquiry, from our response to a lyric poem to our understanding of love, where the discursive intellect will help us very little. Intelligence requires that we recognize this fact and Pascal concludes that 'la dernière démarche de la raison est de reconnaître qu'il y a une infinité de choses qui la surpassent' (L.188, B.267).

Vanity, pride and self-love are further human faults which Pascal, like his contemporary La Rochefoucauld, underlines. Of vanity he writes: 'L'orgueil nous tient d'une possession si naturelle au milieu de nos misères, erreur, etc. Nous perdons encore la vie avec joie pourvu qu'on en parle' (L.628, B.153). He writes a long account of the nature and follies of self-love (L.978, B.100). His conclusion is: 'Qui ne hait en soi son amour-propre et cet instinct qui le porte à se faire Dieu, est bien aveuglé' (L.617, B.492).

Such weaknesses are to be related, directly or indirectly, to the

human vice which Pascal calls 'concupiscence'. As we saw
earlier, this is the traditional theological term for an excessive
desire, having its origin in the senses, for material things and
temporal ends. Preoccupation with the material and temporal
rather than the spiritual and eternal is so natural that Pascal,
having defined concupiscence as 'la possession des choses que la
cupidité des hommes désire' (L., p.368), claims that 'la
concupiscence et la force sont les sources de toutes nos actions'
(L.97, B.334).

And yet, if from one point of view man is obviously morally
weak and intellectually limited, there are features of human
nature which just as strongly compel our admiration. Not least
among these is the fact that man is capable of self-criticism; that
he has an acute awareness of his own faults and limitations: 'La
grandeur de l'homme est grande en ce qu'il se connaît misérable;
un arbre ne se connaît pas misérable' (L.114, B.397). More
generally, consciousness and self-awareness are signal marks of
man's potential greatness. This is a point which Camus was to
make in our own day on the subject of Sisyphus forever striving
to roll his boulder to the top of the slope. At a physical level, the
boulder always wins, but Sisyphus has an awareness of his
defeat while the boulder has no consciousness of its victory.
Camus concludes that 'il faut imaginer Sisyphe heureux'.[3]
Pascal uses the same argument when he defines man as a 'roseau
pensant'. Man has the physical weakness of a reed, but has the
intellectual and moral strength of understanding and awareness:
'Par l'espace l'univers me comprend et m'engloutit comme un
point: par la pensée je le comprends' (L.113, B.348). The effect
of this comment depends on our understanding of the two
different uses of the verb 'comprendre'; the same idea is
conveyed without any potential ambiguity in the other 'roseau
pensant' fragment: 'Mais quand l'univers l'écraserait, l'homme
serait encore plus noble que ce qui le tue, puisqu'il sait qu'il
meurt et l'avantage que l'univers a sur lui. L'univers n'en sait
rien' (L.200, B.347).

The links between awareness, understanding and thought are

[3]Albert Camus, *Le Mythe de Sisyphe*, Paris, Gallimard (Coll. Soleil), 1961
(originally published 1942), p.166.

necessarily close. Consequently, although Pascal points to the limitations of human reason, he still regards the capacity for thought and the reasoning powers of man as another feature of his greatness. He was no anti-rationalist or anti-intellectual. Although he held it to be a rational act to recognize the limits of pure rationality, he could continue in the last passage quoted above: 'Toute notre dignité consiste donc en la pensée'. Elsewhere he says quite clearly: 'Pensée fait la grandeur de l'homme' (L.759, B.346).

The capacity of man to conceive of something totally beyond himself as a source of true happiness (L.143, B.464), and his ability to perform actions prompted by altruism despite his self-love (L.118, B.402), are further proofs of his greatness. So too is the desire for knowledge and truth which Pascal regards as characteristic of human beings. He goes so far as to claim that 'nous sommes incapables de ne pas souhaiter la vérité' (L.401, B.437). Indeed he says that we are beings of such total moral conviction on occasion that we hold certain truths to be proof against all sceptical objection (L.406, B.395). It is sometimes in this way that the heart, as the seat of intelligence, intuition and will, can aspire to knowledge beyond the reach of purely rational deduction (L.423, B.277). It is because of these elements of greatness, and because of the weaknesses and faults with which they co-exist, that Pascal speaks of the 'guerre intestine' experienced by human beings at both the moral and intellectual levels (L.621, B.412). He sets this out clearly in a *pensée* from which a phrase was quoted earlier in this paragraph:

Nous souhaitons la vérité et ne trouvons en nous qu'incertitude.

Nous recherchons le bonheur et ne trouvons que misère et mort.

Nous sommes incapables de ne pas souhaiter la vérité et le bonheur et sommes incapables ni de certitude ni de bonheur.

Pascal makes his own position clear in relation to the doctrines of stoicism and scepticism when he says that he rejects both exclusive praise and exclusive blame of man (L.405, B.421).

As regards the second aspect of man's nature, the social/political, Pascal is not so much concerned to point up contradictions as to show the fragile nature of many social relationships and the fundamental unsatisfactoriness of various legal and political concepts. The *Pensées* do not contain a carefully worked out sociology or a political theory, but they do express some radical views on social, legal and political questions. This is probably the area of his thought where Pascal's analytical scepticism is most apparent. The fact that he produces a penetrating critique of the society of his day is partly a result of his relative scorn for the world of social and political action which he places in the lowest of his 'three orders' since they mostly have to do with 'les grands de la terre' — kings, princes, judges, merchants and other 'rois de concupiscence'. His scepticism, of course, is not exclusively intellectual but has much to do with his belief that both thought and action in society are undermined, and destined to final failure, by the corruption of human nature. This is why he says that the only genuinely effective prescription for society is contained in the two commandments (Matthew 22: 35-40) requiring us to love God and our neighbour (L.376, B.484).

Pascal declares that the different social ranks in society are arbitrary — the outcome of chance, not justice. Far from seeing a close relationship between social status and moral worth, he distinguishes clearly between 'grandeurs d'établissement' and 'grandeurs naturelles' in the second of his *Trois Discours sur les grands*. Indeed, he claims in a brief and pungent sentence that social rank and the ability to govern have no necessary connection: 'On ne choisit pas pour gouverner un vaisseau celui des voyageurs qui est de la meilleure maison' (L.30, B.320). Nevertheless, he goes on to say that in practice we must acknowledge social distinction by whatever ceremonial response is required, but in doing so we are acknowledging the office rather than the man — who may or may not merit respect. Indeed, the fragile authority of the great in the land is confirmed by their dependence on outward trappings, and this is true of judges and doctors, as well as of merchants and princes. They rely heavily on the fact that so many people are impressed by appearance:

> Nos magistrats ont bien connu ce mystère. Leurs robes rouges, leurs hermines dont ils s'emmaillotent en chaffourés, les palais où ils jugent, les fleurs de lys, tout cet appareil auguste était fort nécessaire, et si les médecins n'avaient des soutanes et des mules, et que les docteurs n'eussent des bonnets carrés et des robes trop amples de quatre parties, jamais ils n'auraient dupé le monde qui ne peut résister à cette montre si authentique. S'ils avaient la véritable justice, et si les médecins avaient le vrai art de guérir, ils n'auraient que faire de bonnets carrés (L.44, B.82).

Furthermore, since rank and wealth usually go together, Pascal regards the possession of money or property as being just as arbitrary as the enjoyment of exalted status. Neither can be given a theoretical foundation that is genuinely rational even if both must be appropriately acknowledged in practice.

The structure of human society is therefore arbitrary in this sense. At the same time its laws and customs are extremely relative in both time and place. On this subject Pascal derived some of his ideas, as well as some of his examples, from Montaigne. If human society were governed by laws and customs rooted in absolute truth rather than designed to serve the purposes of those who rule, they would be alike in different places and at different historical periods. But in fact one of the most striking things about them is their unstable and changing nature:

> L'éclat de la véritable équité aurait assujetti tous les peuples. Et les législateurs n'auraient pas pris pour modèle, au lieu de cette justice constante, les fantaisies et les caprices des perses et allemands. On la verrait plantée par tous les états du monde, et dans tous les temps, au lieu qu'on ne voit rien de juste ou d'injuste qui ne change de qualité en changeant de climat, trois degrés d'élévation du pôle renversent toute la jurisprudence, un méridien décide

de la vérité. En peu d'années de possession les lois
fondamentales changent, le droit a ses époques, l'entrée de
Saturne au Lion nous marque l'origine d'un tel crime.
Plaisante justice qu'une rivière borne. Vérité au-deçà des
Pyrénées, erreur au-delà (L.60, B.294).

Pascal insists that it is largely habit and familiarity, not
inherent truth or absolute justice, which ensure that the (wholly
relative) laws of the land are accepted by the majority of citizens
(L.525, B.325). But if simple, ordinary people bow to the law, as
they do to their 'betters', for no good theoretical reason, they
are right at the practical level to do so since the only alternative
that Pascal sees is anarchy and civil war. He is in no doubt that
'le plus grand des maux est les guerres civiles' (L.94, B.313). In
this same fragment he argues that civil war is inevitable if one
really attempts to recompense individual merit since all will
claim merit and fight each other for what they regard as their
due, whereas 'le mal à craindre d'un sot qui succède par droit de
naissance n'est ni si grand, ni si sûr'.

On the subject of state justice Pascal is equally cynical. It is
clear that justice needs to be backed by power and authority,
even by force, if it is to be obeyed in practice. Justice and the
power necessary to enforce it must be linked together. But
justice and force are, in themselves, conflicting concepts. Might
is certainly not judicial right. In Pascal's view men found
themselves unable to maintain justice with sufficient force.
What they did in the end was to exercise force and call it justice.
As he puts it: '… ne pouvant faire que ce qui est juste fût fort,
on a fait que ce qui est fort fût juste' (L.l03, B. 298).

It is clear, then, that Pascal was under no illusion concerning
the theoretical basis of the hierarchical and authoritarian society
of his day. He understood better than most the very
questionable nature of power in seventeenth-century France. He
saw through the paradox of an authority maintained with
considerable severity and inflexibility yet based on the most
brittle of theoretical foundations. Those who exercise power do
so on a conscious principle of deceit and argue as follows: 'Il est
dangereux de dire au peuple que les lois ne sont pas justes, car il

n'y obéit qu'à cause qu'il les croit justes. C'est pourquoi il faut lui dire en même temps qu'il y faut obéir parce qu'elles sont lois, comme il faut obéir aux supérieurs non pas parce qu'ils sont justes, mais parce qu'ils sont supérieurs. Par là voilà toute sédition prévenue, si on peut faire entendre cela et que proprement (c'est) la définition de la justice' (L.66, B.326). A particular form of authority is imposed by exploiting habit, traditional respect, or fear of something worse.

If Pascal understands this so clearly and yet accepts it, is he not a machiavellian in politics? No doubt he would be if his aim were to strengthen and extend the power of those who rule. But this is not his aim. On the contrary, he scorns temporal power. He seems to accept the very falseness which he has exposed for a mixture of reasons. On the one hand, he is not prepared to accept the violence that the destruction of an authoritarian society would necessitate. And he is all the less prepared to accept it since it would end at best in a new set of social and political arrangements equally corrupted by human faults and weaknesses. Man cannot create a truly just society by his own unaided means. The highest goals of political action will always be undermined by various manifestations of concupiscence. On the other hand, he also sympathizes with the view that the structure of a given society represents God's will for man, even when it involves suffering and injustice. Indeed, he appears to have some sympathy with the idea that the *honnête homme* (as his friend Méré argued) should submit to the prevailing political powers and accept his place in an established social order. Not least, Pascal held firmly to the Augustinian view that man cannot fulfil himself and his highest ideals through the state. Because social and political action is purely secular it can never satisfy man's desire for perfection and truth, let alone for happiness. It may temporarily rearrange some elements in the surface pattern of his dilemma; it will certainly not solve it. Pascal wanted a more determined pursuit of moral ends in society, but he was under no illusion that this would bring man true satisfaction.

The third aspect of man's nature examined by Pascal is the metaphysical, or the question of the human condition. It is not always easy to be quite sure about his views on this subject since some of his statements may have been intended for attribution to his *libertin* opponents in passages of dialogue. Also, we need to remember throughout that he is not describing what he thinks man's true situation to be (this is expressed by the fourth, 'theological' aspect) but rather the condition of 'man without God'.

He sees man as a tiny but apparently unique creature lost in a vast and impersonal universe. He writes against the background of the seventeenth-century scientific revolution and is particularly aware of the new perspectives opened up by the discoveries of the telescope and the microscope. The old view of man and his world as being at the centre of things had been overturned. The medieval concept of the closed world had given way to the Renaissance revelation of the infinite universe. Hence Pascal's account of what he terms the 'disproportion' of man. It is something which sets man over against nature rather than integrating him into the natural order.

In one of his longest *pensées* (L.199, B.72) Pascal makes this preliminary point and then emphasizes what a mere speck man is against the vastness of space — not only the vastness visible to human scrutiny but an infinitely greater vastness existing beyond the power of the telescope and which our minds fail to comprehend. He says that our imagination 'se lassera plutôt de concevoir que la nature de fournir' and continues: 'Tout le monde visible n'est qu'un trait imperceptible dans l'ample sein de la nature. Nulle idée n'en approche, nous avons beau enfler nos conceptions au-delà des espaces imaginables, nous n'enfantons que des atomes au prix de la réalité des choses. C'est une sphère infinie dont le centre est partout, la circonférence nulle part'. The contemplation of these facts should teach man humility and give him a more realistic sense of his own limitations.

In order to show further how totally isolated man is, Pascal turns to a reverse comparison between the human scale of things and the infinite smallness of the microcellular structure of matter. The microscope reveals an unending series of miniature universes each smaller than the previous one (just as the telescope reveals an unending series of huge universes each greater than the previous one). Pascal explains his purpose in bringing infinite smallness to man's attention: 'Je lui veux peindre non seulement l'univers visible, mais l'immensité qu'on peut concevoir de la nature dans l'enceinte de ce raccourci d'atome, qu'il y voie une infinité d'univers, dont chacun a son firmament, ses planètes, sa terre, en la même proportion que le monde visible, dans cette terre des animaux, et enfin des cirons dans lesquels il retrouvera ce que les premiers ont donné, et trouvant encore dans les autres la même chose sans fin et sans repos, qu'il se perdra dans ces merveilles aussi étonnantes dans leur petitesse que les autres par leur étendue...' In this way man is shown to be isolated between two infinite abysses which exceed his understanding and his imagination. Hence Pascal's 'metaphysical' definition of man as 'un néant à l'égard de l'infini, un tout à l'égard du néant, un milieu entre rien et tout'. And the epistemological conclusion which he draws is that the human intellect can only light up a very restricted area of reality. Without divine aid it cannot grasp either basic principles or ultimate meanings and purposes. There can be no certainty or finality in human knowledge. Our minds have similar limitations in the intellectual sphere to those which afflict our bodies in the physical world. We are by no means wholly ignorant, but neither do we have complete and certain understanding. And so one of Pascal's most striking accounts of the human condition reads as follows:

Nous voguons sur un milieu vaste, toujours incertains et flottants, poussés d'un bout vers l'autre; quelque terme où nous pensions nous attacher et nous affermir, il branle, et nous quitte, et si nous le suivons il échappe à nos prises, nous glisse et fuit d'une fuite éternelle; rien ne s'arrête pour nous. C'est l'état qui nous est naturel et toutefois le plus contraire à notre inclination. Nous brûlons du désir de trouver une assiette ferme, et une dernière base constante pour y édifier une tour qui s'élève à (l')infini, mais tout notre fondement craque et la terre s'ouvre jusqu'aux abîmes.

This sense of insecurity and instability in human experience forms a sharp contrast with the relative fixity and immutability of the natural world. And a sense of the infinities which exceed our grasp, if it is genuine and deep, will make all finite things appear — relatively — of equal unimportance. It does not matter, on any infinite scale, that we should occupy one rank rather than another. The addition of a few years to our life seems of little or no importance in the perspective of eternity.

This last comment points towards another basic element of the human condition — man's mortality. Pascal has a very sharp sense of the short duration of human life and his description of death, as understood by the non-believer, has a stark and savage ring: 'Le dernier acte est sanglant quelque belle que soit la comédie en tout le reste. On jette enfin de la terre sur la tête et en voilà pour jamais' (L.165, B.210). He also puts together the severe limitations of the human intellect set out above with the fact of inevitable death. The result is a further striking account of the human condition: 'Qu'on s'imagine un nombre d'hommes dans les chaînes, et tous condamnés à la mort, dont les uns étant chaque jour égorgés à la vue des autres, ceux qui restent voient leur propre condition dans celle de leurs semblables, et, se regardant les uns et les autres avec douleur et sans espérance, attendent à leur tour. C'est l'image de la condition des hommes' (L.434, B.199). This is close to one form of the 'absurd' discussed in our own day by Malraux, Camus, and other writers.

Having shown man without God to be lost in a universe which he cannot comprehend and condemned to a death which he cannot avoid, Pascal mentions a third element of the human condition — the purely contingent nature of man. The individual is not a 'necessary' being in the philosophical sense of the term, but a product of biological chance. He finds himself in a silent, indifferent universe without knowing how human beings came to be there, what their purpose is, or what will become of them when they die (L.198, B.693). A suggestion of contingency is contained in the description of man as '*égaré* dans ce recoin de l'univers'. This sense of his own unjustified existence, which the *libertin* must feel acutely when he thinks about such things, is more explicit in the statement: '... je m'effraye et m'étonne de me voir ici plutôt que là, car il n'y a point de raison pourquoi ici plutôt que là, pourquoi à présent plutôt que lors. Qui m'y a mis? Par l'ordre et la conduite de qui ce lieu et ce temps a(-t-)il été destiné à moi?' (L.68, B.205). Elsewhere Pascal writes even more clearly: '...moi qui pense n'aurais point été, si ma mère eût été tuée avant que j'eusse été animé, donc je ne suis pas un être nécessaire' (L.135, B.469). This idea corresponds to the very special concept of the 'absurd' which Sartre expressed and which differs markedly from that of Malraux and Camus. Sartre was referring to this same sense of philosophical contingency and absence of necessity when he wrote — speaking of both natural objects and people — that 'les existants ... se laissent *rencontrer*, mais on ne peut jamais les déduire'.[4] At the metaphysical level, therefore, Pascal sees man as alone in a silent, alien universe, incapable of understanding more than a small segment of his existence, destined to die, and lacking all philosophical necessity.

This metaphysical account of the human condition is used by Pascal to explain a major psychological characteristic of man not mentioned earlier. This is the tendency of so many human beings to throw themselves into some form of activity, be it pleasure or work, self-indulgence or self-discipline, and their inability to remain in a state of inactivity or quiet rest. He observes that 'rien n'est si insupportable à l'homme que d'être dans un plein repos', and he explains this by saying that inactivity allows man to have an acute sense of his metaphysical dereliction and to realize the full horror of 'son néant, son abandon, son insuffisance, sa dépendance, son impuissance, son vide' (L.622, B.131). On this basis Pascal interprets much human activity as a way of escaping from metaphysical reality, a form of distraction or what he calls 'divertissement' — a mechanism by which the individual, whether consciously or unconsciously, 'diverts' his own attention from the stark facts of his human condition: 'Les hommes n'ayant pu guérir la mort, la misère, l'ignorance, ils se sont avisés, pour se rendre heureux, de

[4] Jean-Paul Sartre, *La Nausée*, Paris, Gallimard (Coll. Soleil), 1960 (originally published 1938), p.181.

n'y point penser' (L.133, B.168).

As a result of this analysis, Pascal interprets man's active life as misleading in the sense that its ostensible goal and its underlying motives are at variance with one another. This allows him to explain several things. For example, he notes that generally man does not obtain any truly lasting satisfaction from his activities. When he achieves a particular practical goal, he has in no way fulfilled the 'metaphysical' motives which actually impelled him towards it. Therefore, dissatisfaction intervenes and he must set himself a fresh target. In other words, both work and pleasure bring a series of purely temporary satisfactions, each followed by the need for renewed activity in pursuit of new goals. This disparity between conscious purpose (the pursuit of satisfaction or happiness) and unconscious motive (an effort to ignore the truth that satisfaction and happiness are unattainable) also provides an explanation of the fact that anticipation is so often more satisfactory than realization, that 'to travel hopefully is better than to arrive'. Pascal expresses this psychological truth in a typically terse aphorism: '... on aime mieux la chasse que la prise' (L.136, B.139). Another psychological trait, explained on the same basis, is the tendency of men to go so far as to seek rest and relaxation through often frantic activity. In this way, then, Pascal has found a principle which, he believes, will explain the perennial attraction for human beings of such varied activities as gambling, hunting, dancing, war, money-making, sexual adventures, mathematical research, the pursuit of high office — and even billiards ('... la moindre chose comme un billard et une balle qu'il pousse, suffisent pour le divertir')! And he does not fail to make the point that if man's metaphysical condition explains the motive behind these activities, such activities themselves, with the strong psychological urge which they express, confirm the desperate nature of his condition (L.70, B.165 *bis*).

In all those aspects of man's nature so far discussed, the psychological, the social, the metaphysical, a fourth aspect — the theological — has been present by implication. Because he wrote as a Christian, Pascal inevitably assumed a theological view of man even when he aimed at a dispassionate analysis. From his point of view the contradictions of man's personality, the unsatisfactoriness of his social relationships, and the apparent meaninglessness of his metaphysical condition are all negative qualities precisely because they ignore his theological or spiritual nature. This is obviously an essential tactic in Pascal's general apologetic strategy. He wanted to show that a purely secular account of men is unsatisfactory, and ultimately untenable, because it runs into contradiction and pessimism. He could then demonstrate that Christianity solves the contradiction and dispels the pessimism. The theological aspect of human nature implied in this way must be outlined briefly even though it can only be given retrospective justification after Pascal has put forward his detailed case for Christianity as the second main element in his apologia.

The broad outline of Pascal's theological view of man is contained in his belief that 'l'homme est déchu d'un état de gloire et de communication avec Dieu en un état de tristesse, de pénitence et d'éloignement de Dieu, mais qu'après cette vie nous serons rétablis par un Messie qui devait venir' (L.281, B.613). It follows that man must remain unfulfilled while he fails to establish a proper relationship with God in whom alone he can attain to his 'vraie félicité' (L.149, B.430). For Pascal as for Augustine in the famous opening paragraph of the *Confessions*, 'our hearts are restless till they find their rest in Thee'. There are no solutions to the human dilemma along purely psychological, social or philosophical lines. Many alleged solutions are of course proposed, but their very multiplicity and the contradictions between them show how uncertain and unreliable they are.

The estrangement of man from God, which is the basis of Pascal's theological account of human nature, is the consequence of original sin. The story of the Garden of Eden is a figurative expression of man's fall, through pride, from a state of grace to a condition of spiritual loss. Pascal readily accepts that such a theory must seem the height of folly to many (L.695, B.445), but he maintains that such folly is wiser than man's wisdom. It is sin which accounts for so much of the weakness described in his psychological portrait of man. However unwilling the *libertin* may be to accept this interpretation, Pascal draws strength from the biblical assertion that 'the foolishness of God is wiser than men' (I Corinthians 1: 25).

The other theological feature of man on which Pascal places a great deal of emphasis is the fact that he is a creature destined to a life after death and possessing an immortal soul. He considers that the importance of this issue cannot be exaggerated: 'L'immortalité de l'âme est une chose qui nous importe si fort, qui nous touche si profondément, qu'il faut avoir perdu tout sentiment pour être dans l'indifférence de savoir ce qui en est. Toutes nos actions et nos pensées doivent prendre des routes si différentes, selon qu'il y aura des biens éternels à espérer ou non, qu'il est impossible de faire une démarche avec sens et jugement, qu'en les réglant par la vue de ce point, qui doit être notre dernier objet' (L.427, B.194). He therefore says repeatedly in the *Pensées* that he cannot think of anything more foolish than indifference to such questions as to whether or not man is estranged from God by sin and whether he faces an eternal life after the death of his body. The case for a theological account of man, he implies, must be thoroughly scrutinized and examined with the utmost seriousness before we accept or reject it.

5 The Christian Solution

The theological account of man marks the transition from a predominantly negative picture (psychological, social, metaphysical) to a potentially positive one. The first main object of Pascal's persuasive enterprise is to create in his readers a willingness to give some serious thought at least to this positive possibility. We saw in Chapter 3 that he used the 'wager' as a way of appealing to rational self-interest and, more importantly, of demonstrating that genuine neutrality towards religious questions is not a practical possibility. We saw a more explicitly moral element in his claim that only Christianity offers an explanation of the moral and psychological contradictions of the individual. It does so by asserting that the Fall spoiled man's initially perfect nature, yet without completely destroying it, so that the individual gives constant evidence, in moral/ psychological terms, both of unrealized perfection and inherent faults. Pascal accepts that the doctrine of the Fall is a mystery which pure rationality cannot wholly grasp, but he claims that the difficulty which we experience in understanding such a doctrine is still less than that which we face in attempting to account for man's nature without it: '... l'homme est plus inconcevable sans ce mystère, que ce mystère n'est inconcevable à l'homme' (L.131, B.434).

But Pascal does not leave matters there. Christianity does not simply offer the best available *explanation* of man's dilemma; it identifies the means necessary to a *solution* of it. This is possible because man's separation from God through the Fall is not totally disabling. He is still capable of true knowledge of God: '...les hommes sont tout ensemble indignes de Dieu et capables de Dieu: indignes par leur corruption, capables par leur première nature' (L.444, B. 557). Although this potential in man can be fully realized only by the action of God's grace, Pascal believes that much can still be done, at the level of reasonable argument and demonstration, to prepare man for the operation of this grace. He makes it clear that religion must be made to appear not merely reasonable but positively attractive so that it causes men to hope that it is true and to be anxious to investigate it further (L.12, B.187). However, since the truth of Christianity can never be demonstrated in purely rational terms, and since religious understanding is not wholly a matter of intellectual persuasion but requires the belief associated with 'le cœur', he needs to persuade his readers that reason possesses a limited competence and must — reasonably — give way at some point to an element of faith. He does this in part by reminding us of the fact that in many aspects of our lives other than the religious we accept the certainty of many things which have not been placed beyond all possible doubt by the strict use of pure reason. The fact that the sun will rise tomorrow, for example, is not a philosophical certainty but simply a statistical probability. And so he points to the important part played by probability ('la règle des partis') rather than certainty in our lives:

> S'il ne fallait rien faire que pour le certain on ne devrait rien faire pour la religion, car elle n'est pas certaine. Mais combien de choses fait-on pour l'incertain, les voyages sur mer, les batailles. Je dis donc qu'il ne faudrait rien faire du tout, car rien n'est certain. Et qu'il y a plus de certitude à la religion que non pas que nous voyions le jour de demain.
>
> Car il n'est pas certain que nous voyions demain, mais il est certainement possible que nous ne le voyions pas. On n'en peut pas dire autant de la religion. Il n'est pas certain qu'elle soit mais qui osera dire qu'il est certainement possible qu'elle ne soit pas. Or quand on travaille pour demain et pour l'incertain on agit avec raison, car on doit travailler pour l'incertain par la règle des partis qui est démontrée (L.577, B.234)

It is clear from this and similar passages that Pascal was not a dogmatic, much less a fanatical, apologist. He possessed a keen awareness and understanding of the reservations and difficulties experienced by his readers, trying as far as possible to fashion his presentation of his ideas so as to take account of them. But naturally, although he accepted that the truth of Christianity was uncertain, if probable, in purely rational terms, he had no doubts about its inherent, spiritual truth. And in order to move from rational uncertainty to spiritual conviction he turned the attention of his readers to the authority of the Bible. He wanted to show how purely secular reasoning should ultimately yield to the Christian revelation. He made the need for this transition clear in the *Entretien avec M. de Saci*. He emphasized the inadequacy of the humanist optimism of Epictetus and the disillusioned scepticism of Montaigne. He also insisted upon their obvious incompatibility. He therefore regarded rational philosophical argument as having reached an impasse and expressed the conviction that only the revelation of Scripture could open a way forward: 'De sorte qu'ils ne peuvent subsister seuls à cause de leurs défauts, ni s'unir à cause de leurs oppositions, et qu'ainsi ils se brisent et s'anéantissent pour faire place à la vérité de l'Evangile' (L., p.296). This is why the many and often confusing notes and quotations from the Bible, which readers are sometimes tempted to ignore, play such a major role in the *Pensées*. It is Pascal's intention to make his ultimate case for Christianity on the basis of arguments derived from sacred history and dependent on a belief in the total reliability of the Bible as evidence.

Pascal was not trained as a theologian. We saw in Chapter 3 that in his general apologetic strategy he relied to a considerable extent on the writings of others even though he adapted them with great skill for his own purposes and put the stamp of his literary talent on them. As regards the interpretation of the Bible — what is called biblical exegesis by theologians — he was even more dependent on the learning of others, particularly the Augustinian theologians of Port-Royal. Jansenism gave a most important role to Bible reading and Bible study, and Jansenists generally, as against the Council of Trent, positively favoured the availability of the Bible in the vernacular. At Port-Royal Le Maître de Saci was the most outstanding translator of the Bible and commentator on it, and of course it is significant that he was also Pascal's confessor and spiritual director.

We know that a series of meetings was held around 1656 and
1657 at the 'petit château' of Vaumurier which the Duc de
Luynes had built in order to be close to Port-Royal-des-Champs.
The purpose of these meetings was to examine a draft
translation of the New Testament completed by Le Maître de
Saci. Those who attended these meetings included Arnauld,
Nicole and Pascal himself. Further drafting went on in the light
of further discussions, particularly concerning style, and
Pascal's proposal was adopted that there should be some delay
in publication. This voluntary delay was involuntarily extended
by Saci's arrest (as part of the prosecution of the Jansenists) in
1666 and by Séguier's refusal to grant a privilege allowing
publication. In the following year, however, five years after
Pascal's death, the work was published in Amsterdam with the
imprint of Gaspard Migeot of Mons. It thus became known as
the *Nouveau Testament de Mons*. During his imprisonment in
the Bastille (1666-68) Saci had begun work on the Old Testament
and his translation appeared in Paris in a number of volumes
published between 1672 and 1695. These translations were also
accompanied by verse-by-verse commentaries which provide a
very full picture of Augustinian exegesis. Although the Saci
Bible was never given official approval, largely because of its
Jansenist associations, it achieved a status in France similar in
some ways to that of the King James version in England.

Le Maître de Saci's translations and commentaries —
completed after his death in 1684 by various Jansenists including
Thomas Du Fossé and Charles Huret — are in many ways the
key to an understanding of Pascal's attitude to and use of
biblical evidence in the *Pensées*. Saci defended the traditional
view of the Bible as the divinely inspired word of God at a time
when the tide of rationalist and textual criticism was still
relatively weak but certainly flowing more strongly. Isolated
attacks began to appear on the divinity of Christ and the
historical reliability of the Gospel, while there was a more
widespread questioning of the Creation story, miracles, and the
doctrine of the immortality of the soul. These are among the
'raisonnemens impies' which Saci refers to in his preface to his
translation of Genesis — intended as an introduction to his

entire translation of the Bible. The subject-matter of various sections in the first part of this preface recalls some major topics in the *Pensées*: the authority of Moses confirmed by his miracles; his prophecies confirmed by Christ and the apostles; the divinity of Christ demonstrated by prophecy, miracles, and the survival of the Church; the truth of Christianity as against the Moslem faith, etc. Pascal's classified *liasses* contain such corresponding titles as 'Preuves de Moïse'; 'Preuves de Jesus-Christ'; 'Prophéties'; 'Miracles'; 'Perpétuité'; 'Fausseté des autres religions'.

A notable feature of Saci's Old Testament commentaries is his division of them into two parts entitled 'sens littéral' and 'sens spirituel'. The literal meaning is mostly clarified by reference to the Hebrew text while the spiritual or typological meaning is illuminated by the teachings of Christ himself as well as by those of the apostle Paul and of Augustine. Saci insists both on the historicity of the Old Testament and on its further spiritual meaning — a meaning which is not always easily understood by men and which must sometimes remain a mystery to be accepted by faith. The Old Testament is an allegorical work by divine intention. This is confirmed by Christ's interpretations of the Old Testament in the New, or by Paul's various interpretations and reference to allegory (Galatians 4:24). This approach is reproduced in Pascal's belief in the historical accuracy of the Bible, together with his emphasis on 'figures' or the spiritual sense of the text. But the balance can be a delicate one on occasions, and he is careful to point out the difficulties: 'Deux erreurs. 1. prendre tout littéralement. 2. prendre tout spirituellement' (L.252, B.648).

It is clear, then, that Pascal's 'biblical' fragments, which represent a significant proportion of the *Pensées*, possess the historical interest of reflecting much Jansenist theological thought. If their aim was to take the interested reader beyond interest to belief, it must also be said that they were based on certain assumptions which were being challenged in Pascal's own time and which would be widely rejected today. In so far as Pascal accepted the Bible as a work of ancient history containing a precise chronology and a literal account of the creation of the world, he was no doubt looking for such things in the wrong place. The Bible is a compendium of spiritual truth, not a technical work of science or history. But in so far as he emphasized a spiritual or typological element, he was at one with modern scholars who would accept that it is only by using figurative language that one can attempt to speak, in terms that are at all acceptable let alone possible, about God and certain aspects of the Christian faith. Christians would accept that what Pascal says about the spiritual meaning of Scripture is generally true, but they would go on to argue that this did not require what he regarded as the confirmation of literal interpretations and historical 'facts'. We need not pay a great deal of attention to such features of the *Pensées* as his conviction, shared with Le Maître de Saci, that Adam was a precise historical person or the Fall a precise historical event. But this does not lessen the importance of his views on the significance of original sin or of such doctrines as Incarnation and Redemption.

At the historical level Pascal emphasizes reasonably enough the 'perpétuité', as he calls it, of the Jewish people (e.g. L.311, 451, 456, B.640, 620, 618) and the Christian Church (e.g. L.281, B.613). This perpetuity means that the Old Testament promises made to the Jews and the New Testament conception of the Church have continued to produce a myriad witnesses — prophets, martyrs, saints, teachers — up to the present time.

Pascal also pays a great deal of attention to the miracles and prophecies recorded in the Bible. He clearly regarded miracles as genuine evidence of spiritual reality and God's intervention in human affairs. And so he asserts that 'toute la créance est sur les miracles' (L.846, B.808) and adds firmly: 'Les miracles prouvent le pouvoir que Dieu a sur les cœurs par celui qu'il exerce sur les corps' (L.903, B.851). It is mainly concupiscence which blinds men to the truth of miracles because it causes them to be preoccupied with purely material values.

For Pascal, one of the greatest miracles is the fulfilment of Old Testament prophecy in the New. The fact that the coming of Christ, and his crucifixion, were foretold by the ancient Hebrew prophets further strengthens belief in the divinity of Christ and gives unique spiritual authority to the Bible. The fulfilment of prophecy is seen by Pascal as historical proof of the truth of Christianity. Here again, however, the distinction between literal and spiritual meanings comes into play. For example, Christ's humble birth and life, in the face of the prophecy that the Messiah would be king of the Jews, is explained by saying that Christ was king in a spiritual sense (e.g. the 'King of Love') even though he was not a king in worldly terms. He was, one might say, a king in the *ordre de la charité*, not in the *ordre de la chair*.

While he took an acceptably modern view in insisting on the spiritual or metaphorical dimension of the Bible and warned against excessively literal interpretations (e.g. L.272, B.687), Pascal paid little or no attention to the question of how far the texts he cites were always intended as prophecy or to what extent the New Testament writers described Christ's life in terms consciously related to the prophetic phraseology of the Old Testament. For him, the Bible displayed a wholly remarkable correlation between the Old and New Testaments. It bore clear evidence of a coherence and overall plan which could only be attributed to divine inspiration of the many writers who contributed to it. He wanted to persuade his readers in this way of its historical — and ultimately its spiritual — authority.

At this point Pascal is close to the final, and perhaps most controversial, phase in his case for Christianity. Having appealed mainly to the intellect of the *libertin* both on the grounds that Christianity makes sense of human nature and that the biblical account of historical Christianity possesses unique authority, he nows turns his attention to the *libertin's* will which is locked in a struggle with his concupiscence. As Pascal had shown in *De l'art de persuader*, an appeal to the intellect is of little avail if the will and the feelings are not also touched. At this point therefore he suggests that the individual, even the *libertin*, must will himself to submit provisionally to the forms and habits of belief and worship. This is what he calls 'preuves par la machine' (L.7, B. 248) — that is, proofs by custom and habit — and he explains further: '... apprenez au moins que votre impuissance à croire vient de vos passions...travaillez donc non pas à vous convaincre par l'augmentation des preuves de

Dieu, mais par la diminution de vos passions... apprenez de ceux, etc. qui ont été liés comme vous...suivez la manière par où ils ont commencé. C'est en faisant tout comme s'ils croyaient, en prenant de l'eau bénite, en faisant dire des messes, etc. Naturellement même cela vous fera croire et vous abêtira' (L.418, B.233). Pascal's confidence here is striking. Also, he regards this as a 'natural' tactic and one that has worked for others in the past. But inevitably, the term 'abêtira' has raised some hackles, though it surely simply means that when the unbeliever acts out of repetitive habit rather than complete rational persuasion he behaves at a level that animals and human beings share. Pascal rightly reminds us that 'nous sommes automate autant qu'esprit' (L.821, B.252) so that this tactic does not positively deny reason but brings into play another natural element in man's personality. It is a tactic which may help the individual in time to believe in order that he may eventually understand.

At this stage, of course, the unbeliever is as dependent as ever on the operation of God's grace. Pascal makes it quite clear that belief in prophecy and miracles, even if it can be achieved, does not amount to conversion (e.g. L.842, 378, B.588, 470). And as we saw in Chapter 3, it is the ultimate experience of conversion, not the intermediate stage of intellectual conviction, at which the apology aims. One is reminded of the apostle Paul's firm advice in Colossians 2:8: 'Make sure that no one traps you by some empty rational philosophy based on the principles of this world instead of on Christ' (Jerusalem Bible). Indeed, Pascal accepts that conversion is finally something irrational, a consequence of 'la folie de la croix'. And Christians accept, by the same token, that their belief must appear as folly to unbelievers.

The folly of the cross has to do above all with the doctrines of Incarnation and Redemption. Incarnation claims that Christ was the son of God, as well as a human being, and that it is only through Christ that a man may come to know God — and indeed even himself (L.417, B.548). Redemption means that God sacrificed His son on the cross with the result that belief in Christ and love of Christ allow God to solve the human dilemma and release the individual from the constraints of sin — in fact, to redeem him. This is why Pascal can say of Christianity that although a reasonable case can be made for it on the lines that he has already shown, nevertheless 'après avoir étalé tous ses miracles et toute sa sagesse, elle réprouve tout cela et dit qu'elle n'a ni sagesse ni signe, mais la croix et la folie' (L.291, B.587). This leads us back to the 'Christocentrism' of Pascal's apologia mentioned in Chapter 1. The person and role of Christ, 'le centre où tout tend', is at the culminating point of the *Pensées*. It is a mystery (cf. 'Le Mystère de Jésus', L.919, B.553 & 791) which only faith can grasp. What is involved is an individual and saving knowledge of the God of Abraham, Isaac and Jacob, not intellectual assent to a philosophical idea. It is a relationship in which the whole personality is involved through love, worship and prayer directed towards Jesus Christ. And it is Pascal's conviction, and his contention throughout the *Pensées*, that only acceptance of God's grace, made available through Christ, can make man fully human.

This high point of Pascal's apology is entirely in keeping with his insistence throughout the *Pensées* that God is a 'dieu caché' (e.g. L.242, 394, 781, B.585, 288, 242). For this reason alone his account of Christianity could never have been a linear, logical argument leading directly to conviction. Because of God's hidden nature and the total gap between rational persuasion and a response of the whole personality to divine grace, Pascal was obliged to adopt a subtle and complex strategy in which the argument operates at a variety of conventional and unconventional levels — the logical, the psychological, the historical, the biblical, the mystical, the mimetic, etc. It is this interweaving of strands of persuasion, designed to bring the unbeliever to knowledge of God, which provides both the immediate fascination and the permanent value of the *Pensées*.

Further reading

On the religious background to the seventeenth century, mention must be made of two very large and outstanding works which remain major sources of information: Sainte-Beuve's *Port-Royal* of 1840-59 reprinted in three Pléiade volumes (Paris, Gallimard, 1961, 1962, 1964) and H. Bremond's eleven-volume *Histoire littéraire du sentiment religieux en France* (Paris, Bloud & Gay, 1916-33). More immediately manageable for student purposes are R. Mandrou, *From Humanism to Science 1480-1700* (Harmondsworth, Penguin Books, 1978), P. Janelle, *The Catholic Reformation* (Milwaukee, Bruce Publishing Co., 1963) and L. Cognet, *Les Origines de la spiritualité française au XVIIe siècle* (Paris, Eds. de la Colombe, 1949). Clear and helpful accounts of Jansenism include L. Cognet, *Le Jansénisme* (Paris, P.U.F. (Que sais-je?), 1961) and A. Sedgwick, *Jansenism in Seventeenth-Century France* (Charlottesville, University Press of Virginia, 1977). Apart from Sainte-Beuve's pioneering work, the history and teachings of Port-Royal have been the subject of many studies. A general work is M. Escholier, *Port-Royal* (Paris, Laffont, 1965), while a detailed and penetrating analysis of Port-Royal thought is to be found in J. Laporte, *La Doctrine de Port-Royal: la morale (d'après Arnauld),* 2 vols (Paris, Vrin, 1951-52).

A genuinely authoritative biography of Pascal does not exist, but adequate accounts of his life, as well as suggestive analyses of his thought, can be found in two general works in English: J.H. Broome's admirably thorough *Pascal* (London, Arnold, 1965) and A.J. Krailsheimer's skilfully condensed *Pascal* (Oxford, O.U.P. ('Past Masters'), 1980). As regards the general argument and apologetic design of the *Pensées*, there is much useful information in Marie-Louise Hubert, *Pascal's Unfinished Apology: a Study of his Plan* (New Haven, Yale University Press, 1952), J.E. d'Angers, *Pascal et ses précurseurs* (Paris,

Nouvelles Editions Latines, 1954) and R.E. Lacombe, *L'Apologétique de Pascal* (Paris, P.U.F., 1958).

The best general work on the *Pensées* is J. Mesnard, *Les Pensées de Pascal* (Paris, S.E.D.E.S., 1976). Other illuminating studies of Pascal's thought include Jeanne Russier, *La Foi selon Pascal*, 2 vols (Paris, P.U.F., 1949) and J. Laporte, *Le Cœur et la raison selon Pascal* (Paris, Elzévir, 1950). On a narrower front P. Courcelle offers a close study of the *Entretien* in *L'Entretien de Pascal et Sacy: ses sources et ses énigmes* (Paris, Vrin, 1960), while the wager argument is analysed with impressive thoroughness and intelligence in P. Lønning, *Cet effrayant pari* (Paris, Vrin, 1980).

The specifically religious content and implications of the *Pensées* are discussed in different but suggestive ways by J. Mesnard, *Pascal* (Paris, Desclée de Brouwer ('Les Ecrivains devant Dieu'), 1965), J. Miel, *Pascal and Theology* (Baltimore, Johns Hopkins Press, 1969), A. Gounelle, *La Bible selon Pascal* (Paris, P.U.F., 1970) and P. Sellier, *Pascal et la liturgie* (Paris, P.U.F., 1966). Important collections of essays include H. Gouhier, *Blaise Pascal. Commentaires* (Paris, Vrin, 1966), and two volumes by various hands published to mark the tercentenary of Pascal's death: *Pascal. Textes du Tricentenaire* (Paris, Fayard, 1963) and *Pascal présent, 1662-1962* (Clermont-Ferrand, G. de Bussac, 1963).

Supplement

Since this study was first published there have been some notable contributions to the understanding and interpretation of the *Pensées*. Henri Gouhier added to his already substantial work on Pascal with his *Blaise Pascal: conversion et apologétique* (Paris, Vrin, 1986) in which he explores the transformation of Pascal the convert into Pascal the apologist. In *Papers on French Seventeenth Century Literature*, Vol. XX, 38 (Tübingen, 1993) there is a very full account of a convention held in 1991 on *Pascal's Pensées and recent critical theory*. Hyung-Kil Kim in *De l'art de persuader dans les Pensées de Pascal* (Paris, Nizet, 1992) examines the art of persuasion in the

Pensées and draws material from Pascal's other writings to illustrate it. Hugh Davidson discusses the role of geometry, dialectic and rhetoric in the *Pensées* in his *Pascal and the Arts of the Mind* (Cambridge University Press, 1993). Jean Mesnard published an updated edition of his *Les Pensées de Pascal* (Paris, SEDES) in 1993. A good introduction to Pascal is to be found in Dominique Descotes, *Pascal: biographie et étude de l'œuvre* (Paris, Albin Michel, 1994). Two important works are those of Antony McKenna, *Entre Descartes et Gassendi: la première édition des 'Pensées' de Pascal* (Paris, Universitas; Oxford, Voltaire Foundation, 1993) and Nicholas Hammond, *Playing with Truth: language and the human condition in Pascal's 'Pensées'* (Oxford, Clarendon Press, 1994). The former work, which is a reissue of the first part of the author's two-volume *De Pascal à Voltaire* published in 1990, examines the debate between rationalism and pyrrhonism in Pascal, and the latter analyses the function of language in the *Pensées* and brings new light to bear on certain key words essential for the understanding of Pascal's intentions. Pol Ernst's original study *Les 'Pensées' de Pascal: géologie et stratigraphie* (Paris, Universitas; Oxford, Voltaire Foundation, 1996), by examining the paper on which Pascal wrote his fragments, demonstrates that some fragments previously thought to have been composed at different times were in fact composed at the same time, thus making it necessary to rethink the evolution of the *Pensées*. In his *Blaise Pascal* (London, Macmillan, 1995) Donald Adamson attempts an intellectual biography of Pascal in order to chart different aspects of his perception of the world.

CRITICAL GUIDES TO FRENCH TEXTS

edited by

Roger Little, Wolfgang van Emden, David Williams